Current
CONTROVERSIES

Importing from China

Other Books in the Current Controversies Series

Importing from China

Debra A. Miller, Book Editor

GREENHAVEN PRESS
A part of Gale, Cengage Learning

Detroit • New York • San Francisco • New Haven, Conn • Waterville, Maine • London

GALE
CENGAGE Learning·

Elizabeth Des Chenes, *Director, Publishing Solutions*

© 2012 Greenhaven Press, a part of Gale, Cengage Learning

Gale and Greenhaven Press are registered trademarks used herein under license.

For more information, contact:
Greenhaven Press
27500 Drake Rd.
Farmington Hills, MI 48331-3535
Or you can visit our Internet site at gale.cengage.com

For product information and technology assistance, contact us at

Gale Customer Support, 1-800-877-4253
For permission to use material from this text or product, submit all requests online at
www.cengage.com/permissions

Further permissions questions can be emailed to permissionrequest@cengage.com

Articles in Greenhaven Press anthologies are often edited for length to meet page requirements. In addition, original titles of these works are changed to clearly present the main thesis and to explicitly indicate the author's opinion. Every effort is made to ensure that Greenhaven Press accurately reflects the original intent of the authors. Every effort has been made to trace the owners of copyrighted material.

Cover image copyright © Feng Yu/Shutterstock.com.

LIBRARY OF CONGRESS CATALOGING-IN-PUBLICATION DATA

Importing from China / Debra A. Miller, book editor.
    p. cm. -- (Current controversies)
    Includes bibliographical references and index.
    ISBN 978-0-7377-6233-4 (hardcover) -- ISBN 978-0-7377-6234-1 (pbk.)
    1. United States--Commerce--China. 2. China--Commerce--United States. 3. Imports--United States. 4. Exports--China. 5. United States--Commercial policy. I. Miller, Debra A.
    HF3128.I472 2012
    382'.50973--dc23

                                                                        2012001407

Printed in the United States of America
  1 2 3 4 5   16 15 14 13 12

Contents

Chapter 1: Does Trade with China Benefit the United States?

Yes: Trade with China Benefits the United States

Trade has been the foundation of global economic development throughout history, and today US trade with China benefits America in various ways—helping US companies be more successful, helping Chinese people to purchase more US goods, and providing inexpensive goods to Americans. China also benefits as its economy and population becomes more prosperous. Only a small group of US employees suffer when jobs are moved to China.

No: Trade with China Does Not Benefit the United States

China's economic rise threatens America's future because so-called free trade with China has really been used by multinational corporations to gain a "free ride" at the expense of the US economy. These businesses have not really opened China to US exports; rather, they have focused on supplying the US market from bases in China, thereby avoiding US labor, education, and regulatory costs. This benefits China and earns profits for US corporations but destabilizes and destroys the US economy.

Chapter 2: Are Chinese Imports Safe?

The Food Safety Modernization Act (FSMA) was passed in 2011 and if funded should have a positive impact on food manufacturers in China and the companies that import Chinese food products into the United States. Inspections and new Food and Drug Administration authority contained in FSMA will push China to improve its own food safety system because it will not want to be on the list of countries blocked from exporting foods into America.

No: Chinese Imports Are Not Safe

Chapter 3: Is the US-China Trade Deficit a Threat to the US Economy?

Many people believe that free trade benefits everyone, but as China's economy becomes more developed, it is acquiring a competitive advantage over the US economy. China's mercantilist policies promote Chinese industries, and US corporations, which have set up production facilities in China instead of America, are making huge profits by adding to China's production and technical knowledge, while harming US interests. The US government must implement policies that promote an alignment between corporate interests and those of the larger nation. Such a program would bring jobs back to the United States and balance trade with China.

No: The US-China Trade Deficit Is Not a Threat to the US Economy

The United States is still a global economic superpower, with an economy more than twice as large as China's, and American living standards are far above the Chinese. However, China is a strong economic competitor, along with countries like India and Brazil. Some economists fear that these emerging economies might grow at America's expense, while others maintain that the United States just needs to embrace policies that take advantage of its innate strengths, such as its entrepreneurial tradition and large consumer culture, as the best means to ensure its continued prosperity.

There are signs that China will respond to growing inflation by lifting controls on its currency. This move should make Chinese goods more expensive, improve the US-China trade deficit, and decrease China's purchases of US debt. For the Chinese, this change will raise wages and move China from a producing and exporting economy to a consumer economy—an astonishing accomplishment in economic development.

Chapter 4: Should the United States Toughen Its Trade Policy Toward China?

US trade policy toward China, which has favored quiet diplomacy and maintaining good relations with the country, has failed to address US concerns over China's unfair trading practices. The United States should adopt a firmer negotiating stance that establishes a timetable for Chinese policy changes—such as currency appreciation, intellectual property protection, and better treatment of foreign industries. This approach will work because China needs the US market as much as the United States needs China's manufacturing base and investment.

US policymakers claim that China's weak currency costs American jobs, but there is no evidence this is true. Rather, the United States should focus on identifying and eliminating a wide variety of Chinese anti-competitive subsidies to state-owned and state-controlled Chinese companies. These subsidies make it impossible for US businesses to fairly compete in China, hurting the US as well as the global economy.

No: The United States Should Not Toughen Its Trade Policy Toward China

A stronger Chinese currency—the renminbi or yuan—would not substantially reduce the US-China trade deficit; it would only lower the costs of imported inputs for Chinese exporters and raise the cost of Chinese goods the United States imports from the country. And although a stronger currency might increase US exports to China, the low number of these exports would limit this impact. Over time, the trade deficit will shrink, however, as US exports to China increase with China's expanding middle class.

In 2010, US imports from China rose but so did US exports. These trade figures are good news because they show that US consumers are buying again and that export industries may create more American jobs. However, the US-China trade deficit is likely to continue until China rebalances its economy more towards domestic consumption and the United States moves toward less consumption and more savings.

Foreword

By definition, controversies are "discussions of questions in which opposing opinions clash" (Webster's Twentieth Century Dictionary Unabridged). Few would deny that controversies are a pervasive part of the human condition and exist on virtually every level of human enterprise. Controversies transpire between individuals and among groups, within nations and between nations. Controversies supply the grist necessary for progress by providing challenges and challengers to the status quo. They also create atmospheres where strife and warfare can flourish. A world without controversies would be a peaceful world; but it also would be, by and large, static and prosaic.

The Series' Purpose

The purpose of the Current Controversies series is to explore many of the social, political, and economic controversies dominating the national and international scenes today. Titles selected for inclusion in the series are highly focused and specific. For example, from the larger category of criminal justice, Current Controversies deals with specific topics such as police brutality, gun control, white collar crime, and others. The debates in Current Controversies also are presented in a useful, timeless fashion. Articles and book excerpts included in each title are selected if they contribute valuable, long-range ideas to the overall debate. And wherever possible, current information is enhanced with historical documents and other relevant materials. Thus, while individual titles are current in focus, every effort is made to ensure that they will not become quickly outdated. Books in the Current Controversies series will remain important resources for librarians, teachers, and students for many years.

In addition to keeping the titles focused and specific, great care is taken in the editorial format of each book in the series. Book introductions and chapter prefaces are offered to provide background material for readers. Chapters are organized around several key questions that are answered with diverse opinions representing all points on the political spectrum. Materials in each chapter include opinions in which authors clearly disagree as well as alternative opinions in which authors may agree on a broader issue but disagree on the possible solutions. In this way, the content of each volume in Current Controversies mirrors the mosaic of opinions encountered in society. Readers will quickly realize that there are many viable answers to these complex issues. By questioning each author's conclusions, students and casual readers can begin to develop the critical thinking skills so important to evaluating opinionated material.

Current Controversies is also ideal for controlled research. Each anthology in the series is composed of primary sources taken from a wide gamut of informational categories including periodicals, newspapers, books, US and foreign government documents, and the publications of private and public organizations. Readers will find factual support for reports, debates, and research papers covering all areas of important issues. In addition, an annotated table of contents, an index, a book and periodical bibliography, and a list of organizations to contact are included in each book to expedite further research.

Perhaps more than ever before in history, people are confronted with diverse and contradictory information. During the Persian Gulf War, for example, the public was not only treated to minute-to-minute coverage of the war, it was also inundated with critiques of the coverage and countless analyses of the factors motivating US involvement. Being able to sort through the plethora of opinions accompanying today's major issues, and to draw one's own conclusions, can be a complicated and frustrating struggle. It is the editors' hope that Current Controversies will help readers with this struggle.

Introduction

> "[China's] peaceful economic rise . . . was sparked by reforms instituted by China's leaders in 1978 that embraced capitalism and opened the nation's economy to the rest of the world."

In the last three decades, the world has witnessed a remarkable phenomenon—rapid economic development in China, once one of the planet's poorest countries and still the most populated one. This process of economic development—aimed at bringing the Chinese people out of poverty and improving China's status among other nations—has been truly dramatic, raising the nation's foreign trade from $20.6 billion in 1978 to $2,973 billion in 2010, second only to the United States. China's gross domestic product (GDP), a measure of total national economic output, has averaged growth of close to 10 percent a year at a time when the GDP growth rate of many other developed nations has averaged under 3 percent. This peaceful economic rise, as the Chinese refer to it, was sparked by reforms instituted by China's leaders in 1978 that embraced capitalism and opened the nation's economy to the rest of the world. This path has allowed many Chinese to greatly improve their incomes and quality of life. At the same time, however, Chinese manufacturing and trade policies have often benefited China at the expense of other countries—a problem that has attracted widespread criticism in the United States and elsewhere.

China's economic rise can be directly traced to major reforms implemented in several stages beginning in 1978. Historically, the Chinese government controlled all economic assets, but reformists in the Communist Party of China (CPC), led by Chinese leader Deng Xiaoping, ousted previous government leaders and began changing the way the country's economy operated. The reforms first targeted agriculture, abolishing government-controlled agricultural collectives and creating private plots of land that could be farmed by individual families, with only a portion of the profits paid to the government. China's new leaders also improved education, allowed private businesses to operate in the country for the first time, and encouraged foreigners to invest in a series of special economic zones that were exempted from bureaucratic and government restraints. These reforms caused a great jump in productivity and helped raise the living standards of many rural and urban Chinese.

Later reforms continued to reduce the involvement of the government in businesses, both by allowing an increasing number of state-run enterprises to be privatized and by decreasing the state restrictions on privately run companies. A Chinese stock exchange was also set up to allow for public investments in these companies. As time went by, even more radical reforms were instituted. Among these was a large privatization program implemented for the first time in 1997, in which all but a few state companies were sold to private investors. Reformers also reduced trade barriers, reformed the banking system, and invested in communication and transportation systems. And China applied for and was accepted in 2006 as a member of the World Trade Organization (WTO), an international organization dedicated to free trade among all nations. Together, new economic rules, the investments made in new factories and infrastructure, China's embrace of free trade, and the huge Chinese labor force willing to work hard for low wages created a booming economy that still leads the world in annual growth.

However, China's rise has not been without problems. China's cheap labor and other economic assets have allowed it to become a huge exporter of goods to the developed world, especially the United States. But the flip-side of this fact is that the United States began to import more goods from China, making fewer goods at home and creating a huge US-China trade deficit. Although many of these imported goods are made in American-owned companies based in China, this has meant a loss of manufacturing jobs for Americans. In addition, China has sought to promote its export economy by keeping its currency low compared to the US dollar and by buying US treasury notes and bonds—actions that keep Chinese-made goods cheap relative to US-made goods, and that make foreign-made goods too expensive for most Chinese to afford. Also, China's government still controls certain state monopolies, including petroleum and banking, and it promotes these state industries in ways that give them advantages over foreign-owned companies. Plus, China's huge demand for oil and other commodities has caused global price increases in many essential materials, sparking global inflation. These Chinese policies and economic threats have long been debated and criticized by many economists and trade experts, but US policymakers have so far pursued negotiations, instead of tariffs or other types of trade retaliation, as the way to convince China to lessen its negative impact on other nations' economies.

Today, economic experts say that China is facing a number of challenges that will determine whether it can continue on a path of positive economic development. A global recession in 2007 and 2008 hit China as well as the rest of the world, slowing the country's phenomenal economic growth and forcing the Chinese government to fund a $586 billion fiscal stimulus program. As years have passed, manufacturing in China continues to stall; the construction boom appears to be over; and property values are dropping. Some commentators worry that the Chinese economy might crash, bringing the global economy with it, but others see no such threat and predict that China's leaders will guide the economy into the next logical phase, which might entail slower growth, a larger Chinese consumer sector, and a more balanced economy based on both exports and imports.

The authors of the viewpoints in *Importing from China: Current Controversies* debate many of the critical issues created by China's economic growth, including whether trade with China benefits the United States, whether Chinese imports are safe, whether the US-China trade deficit is a threat to the US economy, and whether the United States should toughen its trade policy towards China.

CHAPTER 1

Does Trade with China Benefit the United States?

Chapter Preface

Many commentators have criticized the US-China trade relationship over the years, especially the US-China trade deficit—a pattern of trade between the two countries in which the value of Chinese imports has vastly outweighed the value of US exports to China. According to many economic experts, this trade deficit exists largely because China is able to produce goods for sale to American consumers at a much lower cost than US manufacturers can produce them. However, rising inflation in China could soon change this equation. For more than a decade, China's inflation rate averaged about 1.8 percent a year, but in July 2011 it soared to a high of 6.5 percent. Later in 2011, the inflation rate dipped slightly to around 6.2 percent, but this still may pose difficulties for China as well as elsewhere in the world. For if Chinese inflation cannot be controlled, many experts say, not only will cheap Chinese exports be a thing of the past, automatically reducing the US-China trade deficit, but inflation could also wreak havoc on China's social order and perhaps the entire world economy.

Commentators say the main contributors to China's growing inflation problem are rising oil, food, and commodity prices. As the raw materials used by Chinese manufacturers increase in cost, these costs must eventually be passed along the manufacturing chain, ultimately making Chinese-made goods more expensive. In addition, rising food and housing costs have led several Chinese cities and provinces to raise the minimum wage for workers—wage inflation that is also adding to the costs of production in China. If Chinese goods become more expensive, consumers will be less likely to buy them. In fact, some foreign companies who have their products manufactured in China are already looking to move their operations to alternate locations in other developing countries, where labor and other costs may still be lower, allowing them to keep end product costs low. But because all countries face higher raw materials prices, moving out of China may not guarantee a continuing flow of cheap imports. Altogether, this poses the specter of a shrinking US and world market for China's exports—the very basis of its export economy—and a reduction of the trade gap between what the United States buys from and sells to China. If there is high enough inflation, experts say, this could even spell the end for China's amazing economic engine, which has produced annual growth of almost 10 percent for several decades.

China has responded to the threat of inflation with fiscal actions, such as raising interest rates on loans and deposits and increasing the reserve requirements of its commercial banks. By hiking interest rates, borrowing is discouraged and saving is encouraged, thereby slowing economic activity. And by increasing the amount of money banks must keep as reserves, less money is available for banks to lend to businesses, also helping to put a brake on economic growth and inflation. This strategy, however, has hurt many small businesses that desperately need loans to survive and has caused even more financial pain for those Chinese citizens who are struggling with rising food and other living expenses. The government therefore has also tried to increase agricultural subsidies to lower food prices and acted to prevent some Chinese companies from raising consumer prices. These actions have had some positive effects, contributing to a dip in the inflation rate in August 2011.

Although a reduction of the US-China trade gap would seem to be good news for the United States, a slower growing China may have many more negative repercussions. For example, many American companies depend on China's low labor and manufacturing costs as an essential element in their own business plans. For years, China in this way has helped to underwrite global economic growth. A sudden loss of this advantage could mean slower growth not only for China but also the United States and other countries around the world. Also, many experts say that the high living costs and slower production created by inflation in China pose a danger to the nation's social stability. If Chinese citizens react to rising prices with protests and riots, it could threaten China's authoritarian leadership, causing it to either break apart or crack down—either way unleashing instability that could affect not only China's but also the world economy.

Although the future of US-China relations may be quite different from the past and the present, the viewpoint authors in this chapter address the issue of whether the existing US-China trade relationship has benefited or hurt the United States.

Cheap Chinese Imports Have Saved American Consumers Billions of Dollars

The Economist

The Economist *is a weekly magazine based in the United Kingdom that focuses on international political and business news.*

During his state visit to America last week, President Hu Jintao of China offered some familiar banalities and worthy pieties, as this week's Banyan remarks. But he also made a couple of hard, quantitative claims. In a speech on January 20th, President Hu said that inexpensive imports from China had saved American consumers $600 billion over the past decade (2001–2010) and that exports to China had created over 14m [million] jobs around the world.

Those figures were probably provided by the Ministry of Commerce, but I've no idea how they were calculated. (The figure of 14m jobs made an earlier appearance in a 2009 piece in the People's Daily.) In this blogpost and a sequel, I'll see if I can make sense of President Hu's arithmetic.

I've received great help in this endeavour from Raphael Auer of the Swiss National Bank and Princeton University. In a paper[*] last year with Andreas Fischer, also of the Swiss National Bank, Mr. Auer estimated the impact of low-wage competition on 325 American manufacturing industries—everything from cat food to artificial funeral wreaths.

Isolating the effect of foreign competition on prices can be tricky. If American demand goes up, for example, it will drive

---

[*] "The effect of low-wage import competition on U.S. inflationary pressure," *Journal of Monetary Economics*, May 2010.

up prices and suck in imports. One might therefore falsely conclude that more imports equals higher prices.

After dealing with this problem, Messrs. Auer and Fischer estimate that whenever Chinese imports increase their market share by 1 percentage point, American producer prices fall by 2.5%, a more pronounced effect than many previous studies had found.

According to Mr Auer, China claimed a 3.7% share of the average market in 2001, rising to 8.6% in 2006, when their data end. Imports from the Middle Kingdom have grown by about 28% in the four years since, even as America's total imports have grown by only 4%. So let's assume that China has enlarged its share of America's manufacturing markets to 10.6%.

That would mean that China's penetration of American markets has increased by 6.9 percentage points from 2001 to 2010 or 0.69 points a year. If each point reduces prices by 2.5%, then this expansion has cut prices by about 1.7% a year.

What does that add up to in dollars and cents? American manufacturing sales averaged $4,512 billion a year in the last decade, according to the Annual Survey of Manufactures, including over $13 billion of cat and dog food in 2005. The calculations above suggest these shipments might have cost $4,590 billion if China had failed to encroach on these markets. This implies savings of about $78 billion a year, or $780 billion over the decade.

This is all heroically back-of-the-envelope stuff. But by this reckoning, President Hu's estimate looks quite plausible, even conservative. In my next post, I'll look at his claim that exports to China have created more than 14m jobs around the world.

Much of the Money Spent on Chinese Imports Goes to US Businesses

Galina Hale and Bart Hobijn

Galina Hale is a senior economist and Bart Hobijn is a senior research advisor, both with the Economic Research Department of the Federal Reserve Bank of San Francisco.

The United States is running a record trade deficit with China. This is no surprise, given the wide array of items in stores labeled "Made in China." This *Economic Letter* examines what fraction of U.S. consumer spending goes for Chinese goods and what part of that fraction reflects the actual cost of imports from China. We perform a similar exercise to determine the foreign and domestic content of all U.S. imports.

In our analysis, we combine data from several sources: Census Bureau 2011 U.S. International Trade Data; the Bureau of Labor Statistics 2010 input-output matrix; and personal consumption expenditures (PCE) by category from the U.S. national accounts of the Commerce Department's Bureau of Economic Analysis. We use the combined data to answer three questions:

- What fraction of U.S. consumer spending goes for goods labeled "Made in China" and what fraction is spent on goods "Made in the USA"?

Galina Hale and Bart Hobijn, "The US Content of 'Made in China,'" *FRBSF Economic Letter*, 2011-25, August 8, 2011. www.frbsf.org. Reprinted from the Federal Reserve Bank of San Francisco Economic Letter 2011-25. The opinions expressed in this article do not necessarily reflect the views of the management of the Federal Reserve Bank of San Francisco, or of the Board of Governors of the Federal Reserve System. Reprinted by permission.

- What part of the cost of goods "Made in China" is actually due to the cost of these imports and what part reflects the value added by U.S. transportation, wholesale, and retail activities? That is, what is the U.S. content of "Made in China"?

- What part of U.S. consumer spending can be traced to the cost of goods imported from China, taking into account not only goods sold directly to consumers, but also goods used as inputs in intermediate stages of production in the United States?

Share of Spending on "Made in China" Goods

Although globalization is widely recognized these days, the U.S. economy actually remains relatively closed. The vast majority of goods and services sold in the United States is produced here. In 2010, imports were about 16% of U.S. GDP [gross domestic product, a measure of a country's total economic output]. Imports from China amounted to 2.5% of GDP....

36% of the price U.S. consumers pay for imported goods actually goes to U.S. companies and workers.

A total of 88.5% of U.S. consumer spending is on items made in the United States. This is largely because services, which make up about two-thirds of spending, are mainly produced locally. The market share of foreign goods is highest in durables, which include cars and electronics. Two-thirds of U.S. durables consumption goes for goods labeled "Made in the USA," while the other third goes for goods made abroad.

Chinese goods account for 2.7% of U.S. PCE [personal consumption expenditures], about one-quarter of the 11.5% foreign share. Chinese imported goods consist mainly of furniture and household equipment; other durables; and clothing and shoes. In the clothing and shoes category, 35.6% of U.S. consumer purchases in 2010 was of items with the "Made in China" label.

Local Content of "Made in China" Goods

Obviously, if a pair of sneakers made in China costs $70 in the United States, not all of that retail price goes to the Chinese manufacturer. In fact, the bulk of the retail price pays for transportation of the sneakers in the United States, rent for the store where they are sold, profits for shareholders of the U.S. retailer, and the cost of marketing the sneakers. These costs include the salaries, wages, and benefits paid to the U.S. workers and managers who staff these operations. . . .

Of the 11.5% of U.S. consumer spending that goes for goods and services produced abroad, 7.3% reflects the cost of imports. The remaining 4.2% goes for U.S. transportation, wholesale, and retail activities. Thus, 36% of the price U.S. consumers pay for imported goods actually goes to U.S. companies and workers.

The total share of [personal consumption expenditures] that goes for goods and services imported from China is 1.9%.

This U.S. fraction is much higher for imports from China. Whereas goods labeled "Made in China" make up 2.7% of U.S. consumer spending, only 1.2% actually reflects the cost of the imported goods. Thus, on average, of every dollar spent on an item labeled "Made in China," 55 cents go for services produced in the United States. In other words, the U.S. content of "Made in China" is about 55%. The fact that the U.S. content of Chinese goods is much higher than for imports as a whole is mainly due to higher retail and wholesale margins on consumer electronics and clothing than on most other goods and services.

Total Import Content of U.S. Consumer Expenditures

Not all goods and services imported into the United States are directly sold to households. Many are used in the production of goods and services in the United States. Hence, part of the 88.5% of spending on goods and services labeled "Made in the USA" pays for imported intermediate goods and services. To properly account for the share of imports in U.S. consumer spending, it's necessary to take into account the contribution of these imported intermediate inputs. We use input-output tables to compute the contribution of imports to U.S. production of final goods and services. Combining the imported share of U.S.-produced goods and services with imported goods and services directly sold to consumers yields the total import content of PCE. . . .

When total import content is considered, 13.9% of U.S. consumer spending can be traced to the cost of imported goods and services. This is substantially higher than the 7.3%, which includes only final imported goods and services and leaves out imported intermediates. Imported oil, which makes up a large part of the production costs of the "gasoline, fuel oil, and other energy goods" and "transportation" categories, is the main contributor to this 6.6 percentage point difference.

The total share of PCE that goes for goods and services imported from China is 1.9%. This is 0.7 percentage point more than the share of Chinese-produced final goods and services in PCE. This difference is mainly due to the use of intermediate goods imported from China in the U.S. production of services. . . .

The import content of PCE has been relatively constant at between 11.7% and 14.2%. Import content peaked in 2008 at

14.2%, which was probably due to the spike in oil prices at the time. The share of imports in PCE is slightly lower than in GDP as a whole because the import content of investment goods turns out to be twice as high as that of consumer goods and services.

The fraction of import content attributable to Chinese imports has doubled over the past decade. In 2000, Chinese goods accounted for 0.9% of the content of PCE. In 2010, Chinese goods accounted for 1.9%. The fact that the overall import content of U.S. consumer goods has remained relatively constant while the Chinese share has doubled indicates that Chinese gains have come, in large part, at the expense of other exporting nations.

It does not seem that so far Chinese exporters are fully passing through their domestic inflation.

Broader Implications

The import content of U.S. PCE attributable to imports from China is useful in understanding where revenue generated by sales to U.S. households flows. It is also important because it affects to what extent price increases for Chinese goods are likely to pass through to U.S. consumer prices.

China's 2011 inflation rate is close to 5%. If Chinese exporters were to pass through all their domestic inflation to the prices of goods they sell in the United States, the PCE price index (PCEPI) would only increase by 1.9% of this 5%, reflecting the Chinese share of U.S. consumer goods and services. That would equal a 0.1 percentage point increase in the PCEPI. The inflationary effects would be highest in the industries in which the share of Chinese imports is highest—clothing and shoes, and electronics. In fact, recent data show accelerating price increases for these goods compared with other goods.

However, it does not seem that so far Chinese exporters are fully passing through their domestic inflation. In May 2011, prices of Chinese imports only increased 2.8% from May 2010. This is partly because a large share of Chinese production costs consists of imports from other countries. . . . [Researchers] demonstrate this by examining the production costs of an iPhone. In 2009, it cost about $179 in China to produce an iPhone, which sold in the United States for about $500. Thus, $179 of the U.S. retail cost consisted of Chinese imported content. However, only $6.50 was actually due to assembly costs in China. The other $172.50 reflected costs of parts produced in other countries, including $10.75 for parts made in the United States. . . .

Of the 2.7% of U.S. consumer purchases going to goods labeled "Made in China," only 1.2% actually represents China-produced content. If we take into account imported intermediate goods, about 13.9% of U.S. consumer spending is attributable to imports, including 1.9% imported from China.

Since the share of PCE attributable to imports from China is less than 2% and some of this can be traced to production in other countries, it is unlikely that recent increases in labor costs and inflation in China will generate broad-based inflationary pressures in the United States.

In the Long Run, US-China Trade Is Good for Both Countries

Molly Castelazo

Molly Castelazo is the founding director of FutureofUS ChinaTrade.com, a joint venture between the W. P. Carey School of Business at Arizona State University and The Kearny Alliance.

Amid all of the recent noise about China's currency, America's trade deficit, and the state of world trade, policymakers and pundits alike seem to have forgotten a very important tenet that has served, for the last half century, as the foundation of global economic development: trade is good.

Global trade isn't a new phenomenon. It has ebbed and flowed as long as history has been recorded (and earlier, surely). The principle has always been the same: one group of people has something that another group wants, and is willing to give it up in exchange for something that the other group has. It's a mutually beneficial—win-win—process.

While all countries that seek to engage with others have important roles to play in the future of world trade, it is the United States and China who should be leading the way toward a more integrated global society.

How Trade with China Benefits the United States

1. From Microsoft and Motorola to Wal-Mart and KFC, there are a number of American and multinational companies that operate in China and are more successful

because of it (And while these companies benefit from manufacturing in China for export elsewhere, they also benefit from selling to China's consumer market.)

2. Because trade makes the people in China more prosperous, they purchase more—and they purchase, in part, what U.S. companies make.

3. "Made in China" products are often less expensive than products manufactured elsewhere—allowing consumers in America access to less expensive goods, from sweaters to computers.

4. While economic integration may lead to job losses in the short-term, in the long run a greater number of higher-quality jobs are created as a result of integration than are lost.

Those who would say that trade [with China] is not positive are looking at a narrow group of stakeholders.

How Trade with the United States Benefits China

1. China's economic integration—marked in part by the dramatic rise in China's goods exports to the U.S. and the rest of the world—has lifted China's per capita GDP relative to the U.S.' 312 percent in thirty years.

2. Perhaps the greatest benefit of China's integration into the global economy has been the diffusion of knowledge and technical know-how from the foreign-invested enterprises (including American and multinational corporations) operating in China.

3. At the same time, China has made substantial progress in protecting human rights, intellectual property, and the environment. Because economic integration makes

developing countries, like China, wealthier, it gives the people there more freedom to focus on important issues like human rights and environmental protection.

Those who would say that trade is not positive are looking at a narrow group of stakeholders (employees who lose jobs as non-competitive U.S. industries move overseas, for example) over a short time frame (say, the time during which those workers are unemployed as they train to work in more competitive, and often higher-paying, industries). It is true that, in the short run, trade is not always positive for everyone affected by it. In the long run, though, we *all* benefit from greater economic integration.

The U.S. needs to take charge of its competitiveness in a much more active way than it has in the past.

What the FutureofUSChinaTrade.com Experts Are Saying About Trade

Ed Prescott, *2004 Nobel Laureate*, W. P. Carey Professor of Economics at Arizona State University: "Economic integration is the path to riches and peace."

Art Blakemore, *Chair of W. P. Carey Economics at Arizona State University*. "The question is not whether China will continue to grow while the U.S. ceases growing, but rather: Are we going to keep growing together or cease growing together?"

Peter Yam, *Former president of Emerson Greater China and chairman of Emerson Electric (China) Holdings Co., Ltd.* "Both [U.S.] lawmakers and the government must wake up and exert leadership in providing an environment for the US firms to become effective global competitors again and regain its strength on exports."

Clyde Prestowitz, *Founder and President of the Economic Strategy Institute*: America needs to compete. But that "is not about the U.S. stopping China from being successful. It's not a zero-sum contest. It is instead about America doing what China has long done—competing, for its own self interest. It is about America doing what is good for America."

Bob Mittelstaedt, *Dean of the W. P. Carey School of Business at Arizona State University*: "Over the long-term, market flexibility—the ability of the education system to teach new skills, the ability of producers to produce different goods and services—is critical, because in a world with truly free trade comparative advantages constantly change."

Jim Jarrett, *former President of Intel China*: "China will do what's right for China, and that makes sense for them. And we have to do the same thing. Fundamentally this isn't a China Issue; it's a U.S. competitiveness issue. The U.S. needs to take charge of its competitiveness in a much more active way than it has in the past."

The US-China Trade Deficit Has Cost US Jobs and Driven Down US Wages

Robert E. Scott

Robert E. Scott is the director of trade and manufacturing policy research for the Economic Policy Institute, a nonpartisan think tank focused on economic policy and the needs of low- and middle-income workers.

Since China entered The World Trade Organization (WTO) in 2001, the extraordinary growth of U.S. trade with China has had a dramatic effect on U.S. workers and the domestic economy. The United States is piling up foreign debt, losing export capacity, and the growing trade deficit has been a prime contributor to the crisis in U.S. manufacturing employment. Between 2001 and 2008, 2.4 million jobs were lost or displaced, including 91,400 in 2008 alone, despite a dramatic decline in total and bilateral U.S.-China trade deficits that began in the second half of that year. Growing trade deficits have cost jobs in every Congressional district, including the District of Columbia and Puerto Rico. . . .

Job Losses and Reduced Wages

The computers, electronic equipment, and parts industries experienced the largest growth in trade deficits with China, leading with 627,700 (26%) of all jobs displaced between 2001 and 2008. As a result, the hardest hit Congressional districts were located in California and Texas, where remaining jobs in

Robert E. Scott, "Unfair China Trade Costs Local Jobs: 2.4 Million Jobs Lost, Thousands Displaced in Every US Congressional District," *EPI Briefing Paper*, no. 260, Economic Policy Institute, March 23, 2010. Reproduced by permission.

those industries are concentrated, and in North Carolina, which was hard hit by job displacement in a variety of manufacturing industries.

But the jobs impact of the China trade deficit is not restricted to job loss and displacement. Competition with low-wage workers from less-developed countries has also driven down wages for other workers in manufacturing and reduced the wages and bargaining power of similar workers throughout the economy. The impact has affected essentially all production workers with less than a four-year college degree—roughly 70% of the private-sector workforce, or about 100 million workers. For a typical full-time median-wage earner in 2006, these indirect losses totaled approximately $1,400 per worker. China is the most important source of downward pressure from trade with less-developed countries, because it pays very low wages and because it was responsible for nearly 40% of U.S. non-oil imports from less-developed countries in 2008.

Rapidly growing imports of computer and electronic parts ... accounted for more than 40% of the $186 billion increase in the U.S. trade deficit with China between 2001 and 2008.

This study finds the following:

- The 2.4 million jobs lost/workers displaced nationwide since 2001 are distributed among all 50 states, the District of Columbia, and Puerto Rico, with the biggest losers, in numeric terms: California (370,000 jobs), Texas (193,700), New York (140,500), Illinois (105,500), Florida (101,600), Pennsylvania (95,700), North Carolina (95,100), Ohio (91,800), Georgia (78,100), and Massachusetts (72,800).

- The hardest-hit states, as a share of total state employment, are New Hampshire (16,300, 2.35%), North

Carolina (95,100, 2.30%), Massachusetts (72,800, 2.25%), California (370,000, 2.23%), Oregon (38,600, 2.19%), Minnesota (58,800 2.17%), Rhode Island (10,600, 2.01%), Alabama (39,300, 1.97%), Idaho (13,500, 1.97%), and South Carolina (38,400, 1.97%).

- Rapidly growing imports of computer and electronic parts (including computers, parts, semiconductors, and audio-video equipment) accounted for more than 40% of the $186 billion increase in the U.S. trade deficit with China between 2001 and 2008. The $73 billion deficit in advanced technology products with China in 2008 was responsible for 27% of the total U.S.-China trade deficit. The growth of this deficit contributed to the elimination of 627,700 U.S. jobs in computer and electronic products in this period. Other hard-hit industrial sectors include apparel and accessories (150,200 jobs), miscellaneous manufactured goods (136,900), and fabricated metal products (108,700); several service sectors were also hard hit by indirect job losses, including administrative support services (153,300) and professional, scientific, and technical services (139,000).

- The hardest-hit Congressional districts had large numbers of workers displaced by manufacturing trade, especially in computer and electronic parts, apparel, and durable goods manufacturing. The three hardest hit Congressional districts were all located in Silicon Valley in California, including the 15th (Santa Clara county, 26,900 jobs, 8.3% of all jobs in the district), the 14th (Palo Alto and nearby cities 20,300 jobs, 6.3%), and the 16th (San Jose and other parts of Santa Clara county, 18,200 jobs, 6.0%).

- The hardest hit Congressional districts were concentrated in states that were heavily exposed to growing China trade deficits in computer and electronic products and other industries such as furniture, textiles, and apparel. Of the top 20 hardest hit districts, eight were in California, four were in North Carolina, three were in Texas, two were in Massachusetts, and one each in Oregon, Georgia, and Alabama. Each of these districts lost more than 8,600 jobs.

Unless China raises the real value of the yuan by at least 40% and eliminates these other trade distortions, the U.S. trade deficit and job losses will continue to grow.

Currency Manipulation

A major cause of the rapidly growing U.S. trade deficit with China is currency manipulation. Unlike other currencies, the Chinese yuan does not fluctuate freely against the dollar. While the value of its currency should have increased as China exported more and more goods, it has instead remained artificially low, and China has aggressively acquired dollars to further depress the value of its own currency. China has tightly pegged its currency to the U.S. dollar at a rate that encourages a large bilateral surplus with the United States. China had to purchase $453 billion in U.S. treasury bills and other securities between December 2008 and December 2009, alone, to maintain this peg. China has acquired a total of $2.4 trillion in foreign exchange reserves as of December 2009. About 70% of these reserves are held in U.S. dollars. This intervention makes the yuan artificially cheap relative to the dollar, effectively subsidizing Chinese exports. The best estimates place this effective subsidy at roughly 40% of the U.S. dollar, even after recent appreciation in the yuan. Currency intervention also artificially raises the cost of U.S. exports to China by a similar amount, making U.S. goods less competitive in that country.

Other policies by the Chinese government also encourage exports. China extensively suppresses labor rights, which lowers production costs within China. An AFL-CIO study estimated that repression of labor rights by the Chinese government has lowered manufacturing wages of Chinese workers by 47% to 86%. China has also been shown to provide massive direct subsidization of export production in many key industries. Finally, it maintains strict, non-tariff barriers to imports. As a result, China's exports to the United States of $337.5 billion in 2008 were more than five times greater than U.S. exports to China, which totaled only $67.2 billion. China's trade surplus was responsible for 68.5% of the U.S. total non-oil trade deficit in 2008, making the China trade relationship this country's most unbalanced by far.

Unless China raises the real value of the yuan by at least 40% and eliminates these other trade distortions, the U.S. trade deficit and job losses will continue to grow rapidly in the future. . . .

China's entry into the WTO was supposed to bring it into compliance with an enforceable, rules-based regime that would require that it open its markets to imports from the United States and other nations. The United States also negotiated a series of special safeguard measures designed to limit the disruptive effects of surging Chinese imports on domestic producers. However, the core of the agreement failed to include any protections to maintain or improve labor or environmental standards and, prior to 2007, the administration rejected all requests for special safeguards protection. In September 2009, the [Barack] Obama administration announced that it would take action to restrict imports of Chinese tires for three years under the special safeguard measures, the first time since 2001 that these measures had been utilized.

China's entry into the WTO has further tilted the international economic playing field against domestic workers and firms and in favor of multinational companies from the United

States and other countries as well as state- and privately owned exporters in China. This shift has increased the global "race to the bottom" in wages and environmental quality and closed thousands of U.S. factories, decimating employment in a wide range of communities, states, and entire regions of the United States. U.S. national interests have suffered while U.S. multinationals have enjoyed record profits on their foreign direct investments.

Failed Expectations

Proponents of China's entry into the WTO frequently claimed that it would create jobs in the United States, increase U.S. exports, and improve the trade deficit with China. President [Bill] Clinton claimed that the agreement allowing China into the WTO, which was negotiated during his administration, "creates a win-win result for both countries." He argued that exports to China "now support hundreds of thousands of American jobs" and that "these figures can grow substantially with the new access to the Chinese market the WTO agreement creates." Others in the White House, such as Kenneth Liberthal, the special advisor to the president and senior director for Asia affairs at the National Security Council, echoed Clinton's assessment:

> Let's be clear as to why a trade deficit might decrease in the short term. China exports far more to the U.S. than it imports [from] the U.S. . . . It will not grow as much as it would have grown without this agreement and over time clearly it will shrink with this agreement.

Promises about jobs and exports misrepresented the real effects of trade on the U.S. economy: trade both creates and destroys jobs. Increases in U.S. exports tend to create jobs in the United States, but increases in imports will lead to job loss—by destroying existing jobs and preventing new job creation—as imports displace goods that otherwise would have been made in the United States by domestic workers.

The impact of trade changes on employment is estimated here by calculating the labor content of changes in the trade balance—the difference between exports and imports. Each $1 billion in computer exports to China from the United States supports American jobs. However, each $1 billion in computer imports *from* China displaces the American workers who would have been employed making them in the United States. On balance, the net employment effect of trade flows depends on the growth in the trade *deficit*, not just exports.

Another critically important promise made by the promoters of liberalized U.S.-China trade was that the United States would benefit because of increased exports to a large and growing consumer market in China. However, despite widespread reports of the rapid growth of the Chinese middle class, this growth has not resulted in a significant increase in U.S. consumer exports to China. The most rapidly growing exports to China are bulk commodities such as grains, scrap, and chemicals; intermediate products such as semiconductors; and producer durables such as aircraft. Furthermore, the increase in U.S. exports to China since 2001 has been overwhelmed by the growth of U.S. imports. . . .

Despite widespread reports of the rapid growth of the Chinese middle class, this growth has not resulted in a significant increase in U.S. consumer exports to China.

Growing Trade Deficits and Job Losses

The U.S. trade deficit with China has risen from $84 billion in 2001 to $270 billion in 2008, an increase of $186 billion. . . . Since China entered the WTO in 2001, this deficit has increased by $26.6 billion per year, on average, or 18% per year.

While it is true that exports support jobs in the United States, it is equally true that imports displace them. The net effect of trade flows on employment is determined by changes in the *trade balance*. The employment impacts of growing trade deficits are estimated in this paper using an input-output model that estimates the direct and indirect labor requirements of producing output in a given domestic industry. The model includes 201 U.S. industries, 84 of which are in the manufacturing sector.

Since China's entry into the WTO in 2001 through 2008, the increase in U.S.-China trade deficits eliminated or displaced 2,418,800 U.S. jobs.

The model estimates the amount of labor (number of jobs) required to produce a given volume of exports and the labor displaced when a given volume of imports is substituted for domestic output. The net of these two numbers is essentially the jobs displaced by growing trade deficits, holding all else equal.

Jobs displaced by the growing China trade deficit are a net drain on employment in trade-related industries, especially those in the manufacturing sector. Even if increases in demand in other sectors absorb all the workers displaced by trade (an unlikely event), it is likely that job quality will suffer, as many non-traded industries such as retail trade and home health care pay lower wages and have less-comprehensive benefits than traded-goods industries.

U.S. exports to China in 2001 supported 166,200 jobs, but U.S. imports displaced production that would have supported 1,188,200 jobs. . . . Therefore, the $84 billion trade deficit in 2001 displaced 1,022,000 jobs in that year. Job displacement rose to 3,349,300 jobs in 2007 and 3,440,700 jobs in 2008.

Since China's entry into the WTO in 2001 through 2008, the increase in U.S.-China trade deficits eliminated or displaced 2,418,800 U.S. jobs. . . . In 2008 alone 91,400 jobs were lost, either by the elimination of existing jobs or by the prevention of new job creation. On average, 345,500 jobs per year have been lost or displaced since China's entry into the WTO.

Trade and Jobs, Industry Details

The composition of imports from China is changing in fundamental ways, with serious implications for certain kinds of high-skill, high-wage jobs once thought to be the hallmark of the U.S. economy. China is moving rapidly "upscale," from low-tech, low-skilled, labor-intensive industries such as apparel, footwear, and basic electronics to more capital- and skills-intensive sectors such as computers, electrical machinery, and motor vehicles; it has also developed a rapidly growing trade surplus in high technology products. . . .

China is rapidly diversifying its export base and expanding into higher value-added commodities.

Trade flows increased dramatically [between 2001 and 2008] . . . , especially imports, which rose from $102 billion in 2001 to $337 billion in 2008. Manufactured goods were 99% of total imports and included a wide array of commodities. Computer and electronic products were responsible for one-third of total imports, including computer equipment . . . and communications, audio, and video equipment. . . . Other major importing sectors included apparel . . . and miscellaneous manufactured products. . . .

U.S. exports rose rapidly in this period, but from a much smaller base, from $18 billion in 2001 to $67 billion in 2008. Manufacturing was the top industry exporting to China— 72% of exports to China in 2008 were manufactured goods. Scrap and second-hand goods industries . . . made up 11.3% of the total. Within manufacturing, key export sectors included chemicals . . . , aerospace products and parts . . . , machinery . . . , and semiconductors and components. . . . However, the scale of U.S. exports is dwarfed by imports, which exceeded the value of exports by more than 5 to 1. . . .

China is rapidly diversifying its export base and expanding into higher value-added commodities such as computer and electronic products, aircraft, and auto parts and machinery. The United States has had a trade deficit with China in advanced technology products (ATP) throughout this period, but it increased more than six-fold, from $11.8 billion in 2002 to $74.0 billion in 2008.

The United States had a deficit in its ATP trade with the rest of the world in 2002. However, rapid growth of U.S. ATP exports to the rest of the world, which increased 7.1% per year between 2002 and 2008, generated a $13 billion surplus in 2008. This sector is enjoying some trade success at the moment. However, this small surplus was completely overwhelmed by the U.S. ATP deficit with China in 2008. As a result, the United States ran an overall deficit in ATP products in 2008, as it has in every year since 2002. The U.S. global ATP trade deficit was $61.1 billion in 2008.

The U.S-China trade relationship needs a fundamental change.

Trade deficits are highly correlated with job losses by industry. . . . Growing trade deficits with China eliminated 1,616,300 manufacturing jobs between 2001 and 2008, more than two-thirds (66.9%) of the total. By far the largest job losses occurred in the computer and electronic products sectors, which lost nearly 627,700 jobs (26.0% of the 2.4 million jobs lost overall). This sector included computer and peripheral equipment . . . and semiconductors and components. . . . Other hard-hit sectors included apparel and accessories, . . . fabricated metal products, . . . and miscellaneous manufacturing. . . . Several service industries, which provide key inputs to traded-goods production, experienced large job losses, including administrative and support services and professional, scientific, and technical services. . . .

A Need for Change

The growing U.S. trade deficit with China has displaced huge numbers of jobs in the United States and has been a prime contributor to the crisis in manufacturing employment over the past seven years. Moreover, the United States is piling up foreign debt, losing export capacity, and facing a more fragile macroeconomic environment.

Is America's loss China's gain? The answer is most certainly no. China has become dependent on the U.S. consumer market for employment generation, suppressed the purchasing power of its own middle class with a weak currency, and, most important, held trillions of dollars in hard currency reserves instead of investing them in public goods that could benefit Chinese households. Its vast purchases of foreign exchange reserves have stimulated the overheating of its domestic economy, and inflation in China has accelerated rapidly in the past year. Its repression of labor rights has suppressed wages, thereby artificially subsidizing exports.

The U.S-China trade relationship needs a fundamental change. Addressing the exchange rate policies and labor standards issues in the Chinese economy are important first steps.

The US Relationship with China Is Lopsided in China's Favor

Robert J. Samuelson

Robert J. Samuelson is an economics columnist for The Washington Post *and* Newsweek *magazine.*

By all appearances, Chinese President Hu Jintao's visit to Washington [in January 2011] . . . changed little in the lopsided American-Chinese relationship. What we have is a system that methodically transfers American jobs, technology and financial power to China in return for only modest Chinese support for important U.S. geopolitical goals: the suppression of Iran's and North Korea's nuclear weapons programs. American officials act as though there's not much they can do to change this.

A New Global Order

It's true that the United States and China have huge common interests in peace and prosperity. Two-way trade (now about $500 billion annually) can provide low-cost consumer goods to Americans and foodstuffs and advanced manufactured products to the Chinese. But China's and America's goals differ radically. The United States wants to broaden the post-World War II international order based on mutually advantageous trade. By contrast, China pursues a new global order in which its needs come first—one in which it subsidizes exports, controls essential imports (oil, food, minerals) and compels the transfer of advanced technology.

Naturally, the United States opposes this sort of system, but that's where we're headed. Clashing goals have trumped shared interests.

American software companies estimate that 85 to 90 per-cent of their products in China are pirated.

Start with distorted trade. The *New York Times* recently reported that Evergreen, a maker of solar panels, is shutting its Massachusetts factory, moving production to a joint venture in China and laying off 800 U.S. workers. Despite $43 million in Massachusetts state aid, Evergreen's chief executive said that China's subsidies—mainly low-interest loans from state-controlled banks—were too great to pass up.

Thus subsidized, Chinese solar panel production rose fifty-fold from 2005 to 2010 reports GTM, a market analysis company. Cheap bank loans to solar companies total about $30 billion, but it's unclear whether they'll be repaid in full, notes GTM analyst Shyam Mehta. "It could be free money," he says. China's share of global production jumped from 9 to 48 percent. In 2010, about 95 percent of China's solar panels were exported.

With details changed, similar stories apply to many industries. The undervaluation of China's currency, the renminbi, by 15 percent or more magnifies the advantage. Jobs shift to China from factories in the United States, Europe and elsewhere.

Next, consider technology transfer. Big multinational firms want to be in China, but the cost of doing so is often the loss of important technology through required licensing agreements, mandatory joint ventures, reverse engineering or outright theft. American software companies estimate that 85 to 90 percent of their products in China are pirated.

Writing in the *Harvard Business Review*, Thomas Hout and Pankaj Ghemawat cite China's high-speed-rail projects. Initially, foreign firms such as Germany's Siemens got most contracts; in 2009, the government began requiring foreign firms to enter into minority joint ventures with Chinese companies. Having mastered the "core technologies," Chinese companies have captured 80 percent or more of the local market and compete with foreign firms for exports. The same thing is occurring in commercial aircraft. China is building a competitor to the Boeing 737 and the Airbus 320; General Electric has entered into a joint venture that will supply the avionics, the electronics that guide the aircraft.

America's present passivity encourages China's new world order, with fateful consequences for the United States and everyone else.

Finally, there's finance. China's foreign exchange reserves—earned mainly through massive export surpluses—approached $2.9 trillion at year-end 2010. These vast holdings (which increase by hundreds of billions annually) enable China to expand its influence by sprinkling low-cost loans around the world or making strategic investments in raw materials and companies. The Financial Times recently reported that China—through the China Export-Import Bank and the China Development Bank—has "lent more money to other developing countries over the past two years than the World Bank."

Sticks Instead of Carrots

It's important to make several qualifications. First, Americans shouldn't blame China for all our economic problems, which are mostly homegrown. Indeed, the ferocity of the financial crisis discredited U.S. economic leadership and emboldened China to pursue its narrow interests more aggressively than ever. Second, the point should not be (as the Chinese allege) to "contain" China's growth; the point should be to modify its economic strategy, which is predatory. It comes at others' expense.

The U.S. response has been mostly carrots—to pretend that sweet reason will persuade China to alter its policies. Last week, President [Barack] Obama and Hu exchanged largely meaningless pledges of "cooperation." Alan Tonelson of the U.S. Business and Industry Council, a group of manufacturers, says U.S. policy verges on "appeasement." We need sticks. The practical difficulty is being tougher without triggering a trade war that weakens the global recovery. Still, it's possible to do something. The Treasury could brand China a currency manipulator, which it clearly is. The administration could move more forcefully against Chinese subsidies. America's present passivity encourages China's new world order, with fateful consequences for the United States and everyone else.

Free Trade with China Has Benefited China More than America

Alan Tonelson

Alan Tonelson is a research fellow at the US Business and Industry Council, an organization that lobbies on behalf of family-owned and closely held US manufacturing companies. He is author of the 2002 book The Race to the Bottom: Why A Worldwide Worker Surplus and Uncontrolled Free Trade Are Sinking American Living Standards.

Here's how proud the [Barack] Obama administration is of its own China policy: Its latest major policy pronouncement—declaring that Beijing is not, as widely charged, deliberately undervaluing its currency to rig trade flows—was made the Friday afternoon before Memorial Day weekend [May 27, 2011], once Congress and most of the media were safely starting their vacations.

If only sheepishness portended rethinking. Although the current mold for the United States' approach to the People's Republic [of China] was set long before President Obama's inauguration, Beijing's behavior along the length and breadth of the Sino-American agenda has unquestionably worsened on the president's watch.

Crackdowns on Chinese dissidents have intensified. Chinese saber-rattling throughout East Asia continues, along with a sweeping military modernization program. Even the US companies that have massively outsourced production, jobs, and technology to China are grousing that Beijing is becoming a less cooperative, less scrupulous business partner.

Alan Tonelson, "Outsourcing Isn't Free Trade with China. It's a Free Ride for China," *The Christian Science Monitor*, June 3, 2011. www.csmonitor.com. Copyright © 2011 by The Christian Science Monitor. Reproduced by permission.

The rapid rise and sheer size of China's economy, moreover, make such bad behavior the world's problem. The most pressing challenge: Its continuing obsessions with exporting and amassing huge financial surpluses are again expanding the global imbalances that have already made the 21st century world economy so fragile and prone to disaster. We need to move beyond the old free-trade/fair-trade debate and explain to Main Street Americans why China's unbridled economic rise threatens their future more than its cheap consumer goods help their pocketbooks.

A Free Ride for China

One promising possibility: the idea that the status quo that multinational businesses have created and defend as free trading is really free-riding. The key to making this point stick is explaining how the companies' actual operations and strategies in China differ from the story they've peddled.

If, as these companies insist, their main aim is opening China's immense and burgeoning market to US exports, then current policies are easy to depict as win-win propositions. Pushing production offshore can be portrayed as complementing the companies' American operations, not replacing them. On an economywide basis, even the sting of import-induced American job loss can be soothed by the promise of export bonanzas and those rock-bottom consumer prices.

Free-riding is indefensible philosophically or practically. Unlike the rest of economic globalization, it's incapable even in theory of producing long-term or worldwide benefits that might justify short-term national costs.

But a radically different picture is painted by China's own continuing export orientation, its constantly surging trade surpluses with the US, and the multinationals' own mounting global trade deficits. These facts strongly indicate that the multinationals are focused mainly on supplying the US market from China, not the other way around. And in this light, the benefits of trade expansion look much less mutual from America's perspective.

In fact, it's easy to conclude that the companies have finagled from Washington a veritable business bonanza that depends on leaving the rest of the US economy in the lurch. That is, they keep reaping all the rewards of selling to an enormous, high-price market like America's. But their China supply bases enable them to avoid many of the costs of this market's upkeep. Principally, they don't need to bear the financial burdens of employing relatively expensive American workers. And they can dodge the taxes that pay for the regulatory apparatus, schools, and other public services essential for maintaining the nation's prosperity and quality of life.

This free-rider argument, therefore, solidifies heated but amorphous complaints about footloose global firms that no longer feel connected to their home country. This new lens reveals the companies' investment and sourcing policies as far worse than simple acts of disloyalty. Instead, they're exposed as decisions with specific, destructive consequences—first and foremost, leaving Americans with little choice but to finance even their most reasonable ambitions by borrowing, rather than earning.

Even worse, free-riding is indefensible philosophically or practically. Unlike the rest of economic globalization, it's incapable even in theory of producing long-term or worldwide benefits that might justify short-term national costs. And unlike many ethically dubious business practices, free-riding can't be rationalized as a way to enhance shareholder value over any significant time frame. As even they should have learned from the financial crisis and lingering recession, not even multinationals themselves can ultimately escape the consequences of the unsustainable course free-riding has helped to create.

Finally, this new characterization of America's China trade policy—and much of its overall trade and globalization policy—should be easy for voters to grasp and, more important, actively oppose. Experience teaches so far that "trade" and "China" as such are both too complicated to demonize in American politics, and both in fact require nuanced approaches. Free-riding, by contrast, has no saving graces and entails no difficult trade-offs. Pinning this label on America's China policy could finally produce the change this failed strategy urgently needs.

CHAPTER 2

Are Chinese Imports Safe?

Background on Health and Safety Concerns over US Imports of Chinese Products

Wayne M. Morrison

Wayne M. Morrison works as a specialist for Asian trade and finance for the Congressional Research Service, the public policy research arm of the US Congress.

In 2007, China overtook Canada to become the largest source of U.S. imports (at $322 billion); accounting for about 17% of all U.S. imports. Over the past year or so [2007], numerous recalls and warnings have been issued by U.S. firms over various products imported from China, due to health and safety concerns. This has led many U.S. policymakers to question the adequacy of China's regulatory environment in ensuring that its exports to the United States meet U.S. standards for health, safety, and quality; as well as the ability of U.S. government regulators, importers, and retailers to identify and take action against unsafe imports (from all countries) before they enter the U.S. market.

Warnings, Recalls, and Detentions

The Food and Drug Administration (FDA) in March 2007 issued warnings and announced voluntary recalls on certain pet foods (and products used to manufacture pet food and animal feed) from China believed to have caused the sickness and deaths of numerous pets in the United States. In May 2007, the FDA issued warnings on certain toothpaste products (some of which were found to be counterfeit) found to origi-

Wayne M. Morrison, "Health and Safety Concerns Over US Imports of Chinese Products: An Overview," Congressional Research Service, January 13, 2009. assets.opencrs.com. Reproduced by permission.

nate in China that contained poisonous chemicals. In June 2007, the FDA announced import controls on all farm-raised catfish, bass, shrimp, dace (related to carp), and eel from China after antimicrobial agents, which are not approved in the United Slates for use in farm-raised aquatic animals, were found. Such shipments will be detained until they are proven to be free of contaminants. On January 25, 2008, the FDA posted on its website a notice by Baxter Healthcare Corporation that it had temporarily halted the manufacture of its multiple-dose vials of heparin (a blood thinner) for injection because of recent reports of serious adverse events (including an estimated 81 deaths and hundreds of complications) associated with the use of this drug. On February 18, 2008, the *New York Times* reported that a Chinese firm that produces an active ingredient used to produce heparin was not certified by the Chinese government to make the drug and had not undergone FDA inspection; many have speculated that the Chinese plant is likely the source of the problem. On September 12, 2008, the FDA issued a health information advisory on infant formula in response to reports of contaminated milk-based infant formula manufactured and sold in China, and later issued a warning on other products containing milk imported from China. On November 12, 2008, the FDA issued a new alert stating that all products containing milk imported from China would be detained unless proven to be free of melamine. On December 2, 2008, the Chinese government reported that melamine-tainted formula had so far killed six children and sickened 294,000 others (51,900 of whom had to be hospitalized and 154 were in serious condition).

The National Highway Traffic Safety Administration (NHTSA) in June 2007 was informed by Foreign Tire Sales Inc., an importer of foreign tires, that it suspected that up to 450,000 tires (later reduced to 255,000 tires) made in China may have a major safety defect (i.e., missing or insufficient gum strip inside the tire). The company was ordered by the

NHTSA to issue a recall. The Chinese government and the manufacturer have maintained that the tires in question meet or exceed U.S. standards.

The Consumer Product Safety Commission (CPSC) issued alerts and announced voluntary recalls by U.S. companies on numerous products made in China in 2007. From January–December 2007, over four-fifths of CPSC recall notices involved Chinese products. Over this period, roughly 17.6 million toy units were recalled because of excessive lead levels. Recalls were also issued on 9.5 million Chinese-made toys (because of the danger of loose magnets), 4.2 million "Aqua Dots" toys (because beads contain a chemical that can turn toxic if ingested) and 1 million toy ovens (due to potential finger entrapment and burn hazards). From January 1 to December 2, 2008, around 2.5 million toy units from China were recalled due to lead. . . .

China has announced a number of initiatives to improve and strengthen food and drug safety supervision and standards, increase inspections, [and] require safety certificates.

U.S. Imports of Products of Concern from China

[Various] products imported from China in 2007 . . . have been the subject of recent U.S. health and safety concerns, such as toys, seafood, tires, animal foods, organic chemicals and pharmaceuticals, and toothpaste. . . . China was a major source of imports for many of these products. For example, China was the largest supplier of imported toys (89% of total), seafood products (15%), and tires (26%); the 2nd largest foreign supplier of animal food products (24%); the 6th largest supplier of toothpaste (1%); and the 9th largest source of imported pharmaceuticals and organic chemicals (3%). . . . [Also] despite health and safety concerns, U.S. imports of most of the products listed (with the exception of toothpaste) increased in 2007 over 2006 levels. For example, toy imports from China grew by 33.4%.

China's Poor Regulatory System

Many analysts contend that China's health and safety regime for manufactured goods and agricultural products is fragmented and ineffective. Problems are seen as including weak consumer protection laws and poorly enforced regulations, lack of inspections and ineffective penalties for code violators, underfunded and understaffed regulatory agencies and poor interagency cooperation, the proliferation of fake goods and ingredients, the existence of numerous unlicensed producers, falsified export documents, extensive pollution, intense competition that often induces firms to cut corners, the relative absence of consumer protection advocacy groups, failure by Chinese firms to closely monitor the quality of their suppliers' products, restrictions on the media, and extensive government corruption and lack of accountability, especially at the local level.

Chinese officials contend that most Chinese-made products are safe and note that U.S. recalls for health and safety reasons have involved a number of countries (as well as U.S. products). They also argue that some of the blame for recalled products belongs to U.S. importers or designers. They further contend that some U.S. products imported into China have failed to meet Chinese standards. However, they have acknowledged numerous product health and safety problems in China, as reflected in reports that have appeared in China's state-controlled media. For example, in June 2004, the Chinese *People's Daily* reported that fake baby formula had killed 50 to 60 infants in China. In June 2006, the *China Daily* reported that 11 people had died from a tainted injection used to treat gall bladders. In August 2006, *Xinhua News Agency* reported that a defective antibiotic drug killed seven people and sickened many others.

China has announced a number of initiatives to improve and strengthen food and drug safety supervision and standards, increase inspections, require safety certificates before some products can be sold, and to crack down on government corruption:

- In May 2007, the *Xinhua News Agency* reported that former director of China's State Food and Drug Administration had been sentenced to death for taking bribes (equivalent to $850,000) in return for approving untested and/or fake medicines (he was executed on July 10, 2007). On the same day, the *Xinhua News Agency* reported that the Chinese government had announced that it would, by the end of 2007, complete regulations for setting up a national food recall system and would ban the sale of toys that failed to pass a national compulsory safety certification.

- On June 27, 2007, the *China Daily* reported that a nationwide inspection of the food production industry had found that a variety of dangerous industrial raw materials had been used in the production of flour, candy, pickles, biscuits, black fungus, melon seeds, bean curd, and seafood. As a result, the government reportedly closed 180 food factories found to be producing unsafe products and/or making fake commodities. It also reported that in 2006, the government had conducted 10.4 million inspections, uncovering problems in 360,000 food businesses, and had closed 152,000 unlicensed food businesses.

- On July 4, 2007, the *China Daily* reported that the government had finished making amendments to all food safety standards and had established an emergency response mechanism among several ministries to deal with major problems regarding food safety.

- On August 9, 2007, *China Daily* reported that the government had pledged to spend $1 billion by 2010 to improve drug and food safety.

- On August 15, 2007, a spokesperson from the Chinese embassy in Washington, DC, said that China would require that every food shipment be inspected for quality by the government by September 1, 2007.

- On August 20, 2007, the Chinese government announced that it had created a 19-member cabinet-level panel to oversee product quality and food safety (headed by Vice-Premier Wu Yi) and would start a four-month nationwide campaign to improve the quality of goods and food.

- On December 5, 2007, the government stated that during the first 10 months of the year, it had shut down 47,800 food factories without operating licenses.

- On January 15, 2008, China announced it had inspected over 3,000 export-oriented toy manufacturers and had revoked licenses for 600 firms that failed to meet quality standards.

Despite these efforts, reports of tainted products persist. For example, in January 2008, dozens of people in Japan reportedly became ill from eating dumplings imported from China that contained pesticide. In September 2008, the Chinese government reported that infant formula that was tainted with melamine had killed four children and sickened 53,000 others (13,000 of whom had to be hospitalized). The government announced on September 22, 2008, that China's chief quality supervisor had stepped down from his post over the incident. Other local and provincial officials have reportedly been sacked for trying to cover up the incident. At least 22

Chinese baby formula companies have been found to have tainted products. Press reports indicate that other milk products made in China may have been contaminated as well. On October 15, 2008, the government ordered a blanket recall of all daily products made before September 14, 2008. Several countries have banned the sale of Chinese-made milk products.

International concerns over the safety of Chinese exports may diminish the attractiveness of China as a destination for foreign investment in export-oriented manufacturing.

The United States and China reached a number of agreements in 2007 to address health and safety concerns:

- On September 11, 2007, the CPSC and its Chinese counterpart, the General Administration of Quality Supervision, Inspection and Quarantine (AQSIQ), signed a Joint Statement on enhancing consumer product safety. China pledged to implement a comprehensive plan to intensify efforts (such as increased inspections, efforts to educate Chinese manufacturers, bilateral technical personnel exchanges and training, regular meetings to exchange information with U.S. officials, and the development of a product tracking system) to prevent exports of unsafe products to the United States, especially in regard to lead paint and toys.

- On September 12, 2007, the NHTSA signed a Memorandum of Cooperation with its Chinese counterpart on enhanced cooperation and communication on vehicles and automotive equipment safety.

- On December 11, 2007, the U.S. Health and Human Services (HHS) announced that it had signed two Memoranda of Agreement (MOA) with its Chinese counterparts; the first covering specific food and feed items that have been of concern to the United States, and the second covering drugs and medical devices. Both MOAs would require Chinese firms that export such products to the United States to register with the Chinese government and to obtain certification before they can export. Such firms would also be subject to annual inspections to ensure they meet U.S. standards. The MOAs also establish mechanisms for greater information sharing, increase access of production facilities by U.S. officials, and create working groups in order to boost cooperation. On March 13, 2008, the FDA announced that it planned to place eight FDA staffers in China. Some members of Congress have proposed placing a CPSC official at the U.S. embassy in Beijing.

Economic Implications

Many Members of Congress have called for tighter rules (such as increased inspections, certification requirements, and mandatory standards for toys), and increased funding for U.S. product safety agencies. On December 19, 2007, the House passed H.R. 4040 (Rush): *the Consumer Product Safety Modernization Act*. On March 6, 2008, the Senate passed its version of H.R. 4040 as a substitute amendment (S. 2263: *the CPSC Reform Act*). House and Senate Conferees reached a compromise agreement on H.R. 4040 on July 28, 2008, and the bill was signed into law (P.L. 110-314) on August 14.

Concerns over the health, safety, and quality of Chinese products could have a number of important economic implications. Both the United States and China have accused each other of using health and safety concerns as an excuse to impose protectionist measures and some observers contend that this issue could lead to growing trade friction between the two sides. International concerns over the safety of Chinese exports may diminish the attractiveness of China as a destination for foreign investment in export-oriented manufacturing, as well as for foreign firms that contract with Chinese firms to make and export products under their labels (such as toys). Efforts by China to restore international confidence in the health and safety of its exports through increased inspections, certification requirements, mandatory testing, etc., could have a significant impact on the cost of doing business in China, which could slow the pace of Chinese exports and hurt employment in the export sector. Moreover, international concerns over the safety of Chinese products could prove to be a setback to the government's efforts to develop and promote internationally recognized Chinese brands (such as cars), which it views as important to the country's future economic development. Thus, it is very likely the Chinese government will take this issue very seriously. However, it is unclear how long it will take for the central government to effectively address the numerous challenges it faces (especially government corruption and counterfeiting) to ensure that its exports comply with the health and safety standards of the United States and other trading partners. Additionally, a sharp decrease in purchases by U.S. consumers of Chinese products could negatively impact U.S. firms that import and/or sell such products and may raise prices of some commodities as firms attempt to rectify various safety problems.

The current [2008] crisis in China over melamine-tainted milk (which can cause kidney stones) and the growing number of children who have reportedly become ill have seriously challenged the government's assertions that most products made in China are safe and that an effective regulatory regime has been established.

China Arrests 2,000 in Food Safety Crackdown

Agence France-Presse

Agence France-Presse is a global news agency based in France.

Beijing—China has arrested around 2,000 people and closed nearly 5,000 businesses in a major crackdown on illegal food additives after a wave of contamination scares, the government said.

China launched the campaign in April following a spate of tainted food scandals—includ[ing] toxic milk, dyed buns and pork found on the market so loaded with bacteria that it reportedly glowed in the dark.

Nearly six million food businesses have now been investigated as part of the crackdown, launched in an effort to shore up plummeting public confidence in Chinese-made food products.

More than 4,900 were shut down for "illegal practices", the government's Food Safety Commission said in a statement late Wednesday.

Police have also destroyed "underground" food production and storage sites, and arrested around 2,000 suspects, it said, adding that anyone found breaking the law would be severely punished.

"All regions and relevant departments will continue to carry out the crackdown on illegal food additives and firmly punish criminals and spare no effort to safeguard peoples' food safety," it said.

China has repeatedly pledged to clean up its vast food industry after milk products tainted with the industrial chemical melamine, added to give the appearance of high protein content, killed at least six babies and sickened 300,000 in 2008.

The scandal caused huge outrage and the following year China passed a food safety law to try to allay public concern but the country has since been hit with numerous food scares.

Experts say there are many causes of food safety problems in China, including ambiguous regulations that create loopholes and underfunded regulators.

Authorities have discovered bean sprouts laced with cancer-causing nitrates, steamed buns with banned chemical preservatives, and rice laced with heavy metals, prompting the latest crackdown.

In June, police in southern China detained a factory owner suspected of mixing an industrial chemical used to soften plastics—known as DEHP—into food additives, the official Xinhua news agency reported.

Xinhua said the initial investigation suggested the company, Yuyan Food Co in Dongguang City, Guangdong province, may have imported raw materials contaminated with DEHP from Taiwan.

Experts say there are many causes of food safety problems in China, including ambiguous regulations that create loopholes and underfunded regulators who struggle to keep tabs on countless small food producers and retailers.

In May, China's top court ordered capital punishment for food safety crimes that result in fatalities.

A former pharmaceutical factory worker was last month given a two-year suspended death sentence—usually commuted to life—for making clenbuterol, an illegal fat-burning chemical, which was sold to pork producers.

The sentencing of Liu Xiang and four others, who received jail terms ranging from nine years to life, was broadcast live on state television, highlighting the level of public concern over tainted pork, a staple in the Chinese diet.

A New US Food Safety Law Will Increase Scrutiny of Chinese Food Imports

Marc Sanchez

Marc Sanchez is an attorney with expertise in food and product safety matters who writes a food-law blog on Food Court, a website that covers food-related news.

In January [2011], the Food Safety Modernization Act (FSMA) was passed and signed into law in the United States. This Act is the first overhaul of the food safety system in 70 years and it will increase the Food and Drug Administration's [FDA] authority over food recalls. It allows the FDA to require food producers to have safety plans and it enhances the FDA's ability to improve the safety of imported foods. However, it does not include any funding provisions to implement the law, even though it is estimated it will cost $1.4 billion over five years.

There are several provisions in the new Act that will directly impact food manufacturers in China and the companies that import Chinese food products into the United States. Imported foods will be inspected and subjected to the same standards as for US foods. The FDA now has the authority to block foods from facilities or countries that refuse FDA inspections. The FDA is also required to establish, "a product tracing system to receive information that improves the capacity to effectively and rapidly track and trace food that is in the United States or offered for import into the United States."

The FDA will also increase its inspection of foreign facilities that produce foods for export to the US. In 2010, before the passage of FSMA, only 2% (roughly 600) of foreign food facilities were inspected. Assuming Congress funds FSMA (a big if in the current budget battle), the FDA will add 2,000 new inspectors to meet the FSMA mandate to inspect 9,600 foreign food facilities by 2015.

China will not want to make the list of countries blocked from being able to export its foods to the United States.

A Broken Food System in China

China is the fourth largest exporter of food to the US and it sends us a gamut of food products. China is best known for a string of high-profile recalls of tainted food. It began in 2007 with pet food contaminated with melamine and continued into 2008 with infant formula and milk also contaminated with melamine. China's food production system is broken and in need of real reform.

Foreign inspection of Chinese facilities means increased pressure for China to modernize. China is often described as being in the midst of an industrial revolution similar to what the US experienced in the 19th Century. At that time in the US, there was no food regulation and adulteration ran rampant. There were cases worse than melamine. Lead shavings were added to pepper and textile dyes were used as food coloring. Even after the Pure Food Act passed in 1906, exemptions and a strong industry lobby rendered the new laws nearly meaningless. It was not until a beefed up FDA came into existence in the 1950s that there was marked improvement in the United States' food production system.

The FSMA Will Pressure China to Improve Safety

China is in the position where the US was in 1906 but under foreign scrutiny. China has attempted reform legislation, but its vast food production system remains largely unchanged. If

FSMA receives its funding, it will act as a new push for rapid modernization of China's food safety system. It will place FDA inspectors on the ground in China and it will increase border inspection of Chinese food coming into the United States. There is no way the FDA can do what the Chinese bureaucracy has been unable (or unwilling) to do, but it can act on China's pride. China will not want to make the list of countries blocked from being able to export its foods to the United States.

FSMA also contains a certification program which will depend on a range of factors, including the known safety risks associated with a food product's country of origin. Though, the certification program is still being formed, my review of its criteria makes me think China is likely to make the list of countries requiring certification. I say this based largely on China's continuing problems with adulteration of food products sold within China and abroad. If China makes the list, the Chinese government will likely be required to accredit that the food it exports to the United States is safe. Putting this responsibility squarely on the Chinese government is bound to raise the pressure to modernize China's dirty and broken food production system.

FSMA will also ratchet-up the pressure on US importers of Chinese food products. The enhanced traceability requirements do not hinge on federal funding, merely on an FDA decision on what system to use. Once the FDA decides what system to use, U.S. companies will need to be recall ready. This means they will need to incorporate traceability into their day to day operations. Should a melamine-type scare arise from China, or from any facility, FSMA ought to enable a rapid recall. Traceability will assist in quickly identifying from where the food product originated and where it was sold. Food companies that depend on imports, like all food companies, will want to begin the process to be recall ready and FSMA compliant! If China is identified as a high risk country US companies will be confronted with the additional task of navigating the certification process. FSMA marks a shift in how food products are kept safe in the US with implications that will reach to China.

Jungle of Problems: Beijing's Failure to Protect Consumers

Stanley Lubman

Stanley Lubman is an expert on Chinese law who teaches at the University of California, Berkeley, School of Law.

What do organic foods, the blood-thinner heparin, and auto airbags have in common? They are among the products recently reported to have been counterfeited in China and exported to the U.S. Chinese businesses that knowingly manufacture unsafe products continue to arouse concerns, both in and outside China. Consistent with long-established practice of using "campaigns" to promote specific policy goals, the Chinese government announced a food safety campaign in February 2011. But campaigns are not enough to attack the many ongoing product safety violators and the business culture that encourages them. China needs both robust consumer protection laws and the means to enforce them, especially at the local government level.

The severity of the problem has been illustrated by Chinese author Sang Ye, who interviewed a number of Chinese citizens to illustrate various aspects of life in China for his book *China Candid* (2006). Among the people he talked to was an employee of a Consumer Protection Association in Hunan, who summed up the prevailing view: ". . . the sheer scale of fraud these days is unprecedented. We make fakes, we sell fakes, we trade in counterfeit currency, and we buy imitation goods. Everyone is a victim, and everyone is cheating everyone else."

Five years after Mr. Sang's book was published, the Chinese government has acknowledged problems protecting consumers but faces a number of obstacles in changing the status quo. Zhang Yong, head of the State Council's Food Safety Commission, remarked earlier this month "it does take time and public support to improve the situation." Mr. Zhang is correct, but the underlying issues are even more complex than he stated, involving a combination of decentralization, neglect of social services and regional government reluctance to take any action that might affect jobs.

[A] World Bank study concludes that implementation of China's 2009 food safety law has been poor and that food safety problems persist.

There is no doubt that China's product safety issues are serious and ongoing, despite measures taken in recent years. Only last month the U.S. Food and Drug Administration (FDA) announced discovery of a plot to fake certification of Chinese grains as organic. Three years ago, adulterated heparin, a blood-thinning drug, was exported to the U.S. in a case that continues to baffle the FDA and fuel anger in Congress. A quick Internet search readily discloses reports of a whole host of other faked products: automobile parts, cigarettes, wine, and (just to show how inventive fakery can be these days), counterfeit U.S. coins.

The Chinese government has tried to use legislation as a weapon against violators. Over the years, a series of consumer protection laws has been issued, including the Consumer Rights and Benefits Protection Law, which was enacted in 1993 and reportedly will soon be amended, and a comprehensive Food Safety Law enacted in 2009. Most recently, heightened concern about safety of food and food-related products prompted the National People's Congress (NPC) to pass a law in February 2011 that raises the penalties for food-related crimes and includes the death penalty. In the meantime, companies are reported to be "allocating more resources to product testing and emphasizing high-quality materials" despite added costs.

But as Zhang Yong's statement suggests, more than legislation is necessary. The effectiveness of legal remedies depends on basic cultural and systemic factors that are now in the midst of inevitably slow change. The decentralization of the Chinese state apparatus places much responsibility for compliance with legal requirements and standards on the lowest levels of government, but funds allocated by Beijing for such purposes are often spent on other matters.

Even if there is no Chinese Upton Sinclair likely to arouse the Chinese government and public, the Party-state should have an interest in energizing public concern.

A January 2011 World Bank report notes that, generally, transfers from the central government are "disproportionately spent on urban development, leaving a shortage of resources at the county level and below to spend on essential social services." A study written in 2007 at the Nixon Center in Washington reached the same conclusion, and in addition cited other problems such as the reluctance of local governments to close businesses that contribute to local employment, as well as collusion with illegal or unlicensed manufacturers in order to continue to collect fines from violators. The World Bank study concludes that implementation of China's 2009 food safety law has been poor and that food safety problems persist. The Nixon Center study pointed to China's lack of a "robust and productive civil society that collectively represents the interests of consumers as well as manufacturers." More specifically, it concluded that "without a strong legal system, insurance companies, industry associations and 'consumer watchdogs'" to support government efforts, "the Chinese system lacks many tools that ensure food and drug processors adhere to good manufacturing practices."

To put food safety problems in historical perspective, the 19th century saw American industry, including food manufacturing and processing, develop at great speed and with little regulation. By the end of the century, problems with the quality of meat products were shocking. Public attention was aroused in 1906 when Upton Sinclair published *The Jungle*, a novel that vividly described conditions in the meat-packing plants of Chicago. As Stewart Macaulay and others noted in *Law and Society: Readings on the Social Study of Law* (1985), President Theodore Roosevelt used the book to push Congress to pass legislation that led to the creation of the FDA.

The history of the FDA suggests that public concern and outrage can influence government action to increase regulation of an industry that is injuring or killing consumers. China has already experienced instances of citizen anger that have stimulated government enforcement. However, citizen protests are too often suppressed by local governments, such as the way authorities in Henan in 2008 delayed any response after the adulteration of milk powder was shown to sicken and, in some cases, kill children.

Even if there is no Chinese Upton Sinclair likely to arouse the Chinese government and public, the Party-state should have an interest in energizing public concern. The "social stability" that the Chinese leadership is so anxious to maintain would benefit from central government pressure on local governments to solicit and heed expressions of citizens' worries, not only about food safety but product safety and counterfeiting generally.

Chinese business is deeply marred by extensive counterfeiting of almost anything that one can think of. In this context, the efforts necessary to bring about significant modification of the conduct of manufacturers and processors will have to go beyond mere campaigns. Government efforts should be

directed at raising consciousness over the long term (not difficult, given the ubiquity of unsafe or counterfeit products),
such as by promoting consumer protection NGOs and web-
sites. More basically, there is a need to strengthen local
governments' enforcement of product safety laws by assuring
that they have the necessary resources to attack violations and
use those resources for that purpose—rather than pursue development for development's sake.

The Safety of Chinese Food Products Is Not Improving

Food & Water Watch

Food & Water Watch is a nonprofit organization that advocates for policies that guarantee safe, wholesome food produced in a humane and sustainable manner, and that supports public, rather than private, control of water resources, including oceans, rivers, and groundwater.

China has become an agricultural powerhouse and leading food exporter. Though supermarket labels may not always indicate it, a growing portion of the American diet is now made in China. In 2009, 70 percent of the apple juice, 43 percent of the processed mushrooms, 22 percent of the frozen spinach and 78 percent of the tilapia Americans ate came from China.

Unfortunately, it's not just China's food that's reaching American shores—it's also China's food safety problems.

Systemic Food Safety Failures

The shortcomings in China's food safety system were highlighted when ingredients tainted with the chemical melamine entered the global food supply—including products from well-known brands like Mars, Heinz and Cadbury. Melamine-tainted milk products sickened hundreds of thousands of infants in China, and melamine contamination is believed to be responsible for thousands of pet deaths in the United States.

Melamine adulteration garnered the most headlines, but systemic food safety failures in China have allowed unsafe foods onto global grocery store shelves. The Wild West business environment in China encourages food manufacturers to cut costs and corners. Even Chinese officials have publicly acknowledged their inability to regulate the country's sprawling food production sector.

It is time for a common-sense approach to inspecting imported food and preventing the globalization of the food supply from sickening our citizens.

U.S. food safety inspectors have been overwhelmed by the surging food imports from China since the country joined the World Trade Organization (WTO) in 2001. These international business deals allow trade to trump food safety and encourage U.S. agribusinesses and food manufacturers to source food ingredients in China where environmental, food safety and labor laws are weaker and regulatory oversight is lax.

The [US] Food and Drug Administration (FDA) has done little to address the growing tide of food imports from China, despite a well-documented pattern of chemical adulteration and unsafe drug residues. The FDA inspects less than 2 percent of imported food and barely visits Chinese food manufacturers. The FDA conducted only 13 food inspections in China between June 2009 and June 2010.

Continuing Problems

There is no indication that China's food safety situation is improving. Melamine continues to appear in food inside China despite a spate of new food safety legislation. Nonetheless, the U.S. Department of Agriculture (USDA) is considering allowing U.S. food retailers to import chicken from China. It is time for a common-sense approach to inspecting imported food and preventing the globalization of the food supply from sickening our citizens.

A new direction would include:

- Revisiting the current trade agenda to make public health, environmental standards and consumer safety the highest priorities.

- Removing agriculture from the WTO. The WTO has been a failure for U.S. farmers and has encouraged companies to offshore food manufacturing to places like China with low wages and weak regulatory standards, putting consumers around the world at risk.

- Restarting the assessment of China's poultry inspection system before considering allowing Chinese poultry products to be exported to the United States.

- Significantly increasing FDA and USDA funding to increase inspections of the growing volume of food imports from China and other countries. The FDA also needs the resources to conduct inspections in food facilities in China.

- Closing the loopholes in the current country-of-origin labeling rules on meats, seafood, fruits and vegetables, and expanding the labeling requirements to cover processed food.

Food Safety Is Still a Crucial Issue in China

Cesar Chelala

Cesar Chelala is a global public health consultant and a contributing editor for the Globalist, *an online magazine and website that focuses on issues of globalization.*

The issue of food safety is very important to China, particularly in rural areas that lack control and supervision. Although the Chinese government has stepped up supervision of food and dairy products and liquor sold in rural areas at all points in the supply chain, it has to take more effective measures to ensure food safety.

A large number of people fall sick because of intentional contamination of food by producers or because of careless and unsupervised practices. Some prohibited substances are added to food products to mask their poor quality, extend their shelf life or make them look more nutritious.

Continuing Problems of Contaminated Food

Almost three years after a national health scare over melamine-contaminated milk products shook China's dairy industry there has been a new wave of reports on adulterated food. Melamine is a substance used in fertilizers and plastics, and when added to food products it pretends to increase their protein content during food-quality tests. This substance, which some Chinese food producers added (and some still do) to infant milk products, chocolate and other food, could cause permanent damage to kidneys if consumed in large quantities.

Recently, there have been reports of pork adulterated with clenbuterol, a drug that can cause heart problems; rice contaminated with cadmium, a metal discharged by smelters; soy sauce laced with arsenic; noodles mixed with ink and wax; bean sprouts contaminated with an animal antibiotic; and eggs induced with chemicals, gelatin and paraffin among other adulterated food products.

The most evident feature of China's food safety regulatory system is the fragmentation of regulatory authority among several government agencies.

Rather than diminishing, the problem of contaminated food seems to be increasing, particularly in rural areas. Why? The lure of making easy money is too tempting for many food producers. They have realized that by using additives they can increase their profit margins. The tragedy is that such food producers don't consider the serious effects that adulterated food has on consumers.

China's rapid growth in the past few decades has given rise to an estimated half a million food producers, most of whom employ 10 or fewer workers, and supervising them is difficult because they are spread throughout the country. The dearth of qualified food quality supervisors and the huge number of food producers have aggravated the situation. Since the profits made by adulterated food can bring considerable economic benefits to local economies by increasing government income and employment opportunities, many local officials tend to turn a blind eye to such activities. To make things more complex, adulterated products are not sold in and around the places they are produced. Instead, they are transported to other areas, thus reducing the necessity and incentives of local authorities to crack down on such harmful activities.

Many adulterated food products, such as "fake" milk, are sold in rural areas making many children vulnerable to unknown health dangers. Some analysts attribute the prevalence of adulterated foods in rural areas to the low purchasing power and lower educational level of villagers, and the regulatory chasm between urban and rural areas.

Problems with China's Food Safety Regulation

For many experts, the most evident feature of China's food safety regulatory system is the fragmentation of regulatory authority among several government agencies. This is in contrast to the United States, where except for meat and poultry, which the Department of Agriculture regulates, the Food and Drug Administration is in charge of almost the entire food chain.

China's food regulating agencies have to be streamlined and their responsibilities clearly established.

In 2003, in an attempt to correct this situation, the Chinese leadership created the State Food and Drug Administration (SFDA) to regulate and comprehensively supervise food products. But soon after its creation, it became evident that the new agency would face some serious criticism, particularly from other regulatory agencies. In the following years, the SFDA did not have enough authority to exercise complete supervision over food safety—and its authority remains divided among different government agencies.

The government, however, has made some progress on the issue. In 2009, China adopted a comprehensive Food Safety Law, implementing hundreds of standards of food production in line with international norms. As a result, almost half of the country's dairy food companies have been ordered to stop production after failing to meet new licensing requirements.

Besides, the Ministry of Health plans to update and make public a list of legal food additives and blacklist some additives by the end of this year.

The government has to take measures to educate rural people to a level where they can distinguish between genuinely healthy food products and their contaminated varieties, and demand safe and quality products. It has to train more enforcement agents, too, because the present lot of food inspectors are not qualified enough to meet the demands. More importantly, China's food regulating agencies have to be streamlined and their responsibilities clearly established. A clear division of duties will make Chinese citizens feel that the government is protecting their health and well-being.

CHAPTER 3

Is the US-China Trade Deficit a Threat to the US Economy?

Background on the US Trade Deficit with China

Kimberly Amadeo

Kimberly Amadeo is a public speaker, author, and consultant, as well as an expert on the US economy, for About.com, an information website and a part of the New York Times Company.

In 2010 ..., the U.S. trade deficit with China was $252 billion. This was down slightly from the record of $268 billion set in 2008, the largest in the world between any two countries. The deficit means that the U.S. exported $82 billion in goods and services to China (double its 2005 exports), while it imported over $334 billion (second only to 2006 levels).

Why Is There a U.S. Trade Deficit with China?

China is able to produce low-cost goods that Americans want. Most economists agree that China's competitive pricing is a result of two factors:

1. A lower standard of living, which allows them to pay lower wages to workers.

2. An exchange rate that is partially set to be always priced lower than the dollar.

How Can China Set Its Exchange Rate Lower than the Dollar?

China sets the value of its currency, the yuan, to always equal a set amount of a basket of currencies which includes the dollar. When the dollar loses value, China buys dollars through

U.S. Treasuries to support it. In this way, the yuan's value is always within its targeted range. As long as the yuan's value is lower than the dollar, China's goods are cheaper in comparison.

The U.S. trade deficit with China means that U.S. companies that can't compete with cheap Chinese goods must either lower their costs or go out of business.

How Does the U.S. Trade Deficit with China Affect the US Economy?

China bought U.S. Treasuries to support the value of the dollar, and keep its exports cheap. It is now the largest lender to the U.S. Government. In November 2010, China owned $895 billion in U.S. Treasuries, 32% of the total $2.8 trillion outstanding. Many are concerned that this gives China political leverage over U.S. fiscal policy, since it could theoretically call in its loan.

By buying Treasuries, China helped keep U.S. interest rates low. Until the Subprime Mortgage Crisis, this helped fuel the U.S. housing boom. If China were to stop buying Treasuries, interest rates would rise, delaying any recovery from the recession. This isn't in China's best interests, as U.S. shoppers would buy fewer Chinese exports. However, China is buying fewer Treasuries than in November 2009, when it owned $929 billion. China is diversifying its holdings into other currencies, such as the euro.

The U.S. trade deficit with China means that U.S. companies that can't compete with cheap Chinese goods must either lower their costs or go out of business. To lower their costs, many companies have started outsourcing to India and China, adding to U.S. unemployment. Other industries have simply dried up. U.S. manufacturing, as measured by the number of jobs, declined 34% between 1998 and 2010. As these industries declined, so has U.S. competitiveness in the global marketplace.

What Is Being Done to Improve the US Trade Deficit with China?

In 2009, Treasury Secretary Tim Geithner continued the U.S.-China Strategic Economic Dialogue, which pressures China to loosen its peg against the dollar and raise the price of Chinese exports, lowering the trade deficit. The Dialogue also opens up to U.S. companies China's domestic market of 1.3 billion people (the largest in the world). This was begun in 2006, by former Treasury Secretary Henry Paulson. Since the Dialogue was begun, China allowed the yuan to rise 16% and opened many Chinese markets to U.S. industries.

The US-China Trade Deficit Is the Main Structural Problem with the US Economy

Peter Navarro

Peter Navarro is a business professor at the University of California at Irvine, as well as a CNBC contributor and the coauthor, with Greg Autry, of the 2011 book Death by China: Confronting the Dragon—A Global Call to Action.

The American economy has been in trouble for more than a decade, and no amount of right-wing tax cuts or left-wing fiscal stimuli will solve the primary structural problem underpinning our slow growth and high unemployment. That problem is a massive, persistent trade deficit—most of it with China—that cuts the number of jobs created by nearly the number we need to keep America fully employed.

To understand why huge U.S. trade deficits represent the taproot of the nation's economic woes, it's crucial to understand that four factors drive our gross domestic product: consumption, business investment, government spending and net exports. This discussion focuses on net exports.

The U.S.-China Trade Deficit

Net exports represent the difference between how much we export and import. A trade deficit means net exports are negative, and that directly reduces both the GDP [gross domestic product, a measure of a country's total economic output] growth rate and rate of job creation.

America's trade deficit is costing us close to 1% of GDP growth a year at a loss of almost 1 million jobs annually.

That's millions of jobs we have failed to create over the last decade; and if we had those jobs now, we wouldn't see continuing high unemployment numbers, padlocked houses under foreclosure and empty factories pushing up weeds.

How can we eliminate ... our trade deficit with China? For starters, we must puncture the myth that China's main manufacturing edge is solely its cheap labor.

It follows that if we want to get America back to work, we need to sharply reduce our trade deficit. As a statistical matter, that means sharply reducing our trade deficit with China.

Every business day, American consumers buy $1 billion more in Chinese exports than American manufacturers sell to China, and China alone accounts for about 70% of America's trade deficit in goods, excluding oil imports. This "Chinese import dependence" has led a democratic America to owe the largest communist nation in the world more than $1 trillion, while China holds more than $3 trillion in foreign reserves, most of them in U.S. dollars.

To put these dollar reserves in perspective, that's more than enough money for China to buy a controlling interest in every major company in the Dow Jones Industrial Average, including Alcoa, Caterpillar, Exxon Mobil and Wal-Mart, and still leave billions to spare.

China's Unfair Trade Practices

So how can we eliminate, or at least drastically reduce, our trade deficit with China? For starters, we must puncture the myth that China's main manufacturing edge is solely its cheap labor. Indeed, while low labor costs are a factor, when you carefully research the biggest source of China's manufacturing advantage, it is actually a complex array of unfair trade practices, all of which are illegal under free-trade rules.

The most potent of China's "weapons of job destruction" are an elaborate web of export subsidies; the blatant piracy of America's technologies and trade secrets; the counterfeiting of valuable brand names like Nike and Chevy; a cleverly manipulated and grossly undervalued currency; and the forced transfer of the technology of any American company wishing to operate on Chinese soil or sell into the Chinese market.

The idea that free trade always benefits both countries ... doesn't hold true if one country cheats on the other.

Each of these unfair trade practices is expressly prohibited both by World Trade Organization rules as well as rules established by the U.S. government, e.g., the Treasury Department has sanctions against currency manipulation (which, alas, the [Barack] Obama administration refuses to use against China despite campaign promises to do so).

In addition, there is the Chinese Communist Party's incredibly shortsighted willingness to trade tremendous environmental damage and a surfeit of workplace deaths and injuries for a few more pennies of production cost advantage, all because of ultra-lax regulatory standards. For example, according to the World Health Organization, almost 700,000 Chinese citizens die annually from the effects of air pollution—that's like losing everybody in Wyoming every year—while Chinese officials acknowledge more than 2,000 coal mining deaths annually, compared with fewer than 50 in the United States.

Make no mistake. All of these real economic weapons have led to the shutdown of thousands of American factories and turned millions of American workers into collateral damage, all under the false flag of so-called free trade.

The Threat to America

The second myth we must expose if we are to ever reverse the job-killing trade deficits we now run with China is the idea that free trade always benefits both countries. That doesn't hold true if one country cheats on the other. Instead, when a mercantilist China uses unfair trade practices to wage war on our manufacturing base, the American economy is the big loser.

Given America's structural problem with China and absent constructive trade reform, our economic prospects can only dim further. The presidential candidate who grasps that essential truth, which is becoming increasingly understood by much of the electorate, will be the one who wins in 2012. We need someone who can lead this country to a trade relationship with China founded on the American ideals of free and fair trade rather than a set of mercantilist and socialist trade policies that employ the Chinese masses at the expense of American workers.

China's Economic Development and the US-China Trade Imbalance Is Harmful to the US Economy

Ralph E. Gomory

Ralph E. Gomory is a research professor at the Stern School of Business at New York University. He previously worked as head of research for IBM and director of the Alfred P. Sloan Foundation, a nonprofit philanthropic institution that provides grants for various science and technology research projects.

Many of the questions ... proposed to this panel [US-China Economic and Security Review Commission] relate to China's efforts to move its people into more productive jobs where they can create more value for each hour worked, and to the means, ranging from foreign direct investment to direct acquisition of knowledge abroad, that China has used and will use to acquire the technical knowledge that is needed to produce that result. Explicit or implicit in many of the questions is also the question of the impact of these actions on the U.S. and the likelihood of their success in the future. A further implicit question posed is this: What can the U.S. do when these impacts are detrimental to the U.S.?...

Benefits at a High Price

What we can expect in the future is simply more, and probably much more, of what we have seen to date.

What we have seen to date is this: rapid economic growth in China, coupled with a major negative impact of the im-

Ralph E. Gomory, "Hearing on China's Five-Year Plan, Indigenous Innovation and Technology Transfers, and Outsourcing," Testimony Before the US–China Economic and Security Review Commission, June 15, 2011. Reproduced by permission.

ports of Chinese goods on the productive capability of this county. We have seen an enormous imbalance of trade as these imports are not balanced by a sufficient counter-flow of exports. In the U.S. we have seen greater corporate profits, accompanied by downward pressure on wages and employment.

While the inflow of cheaper consumer goods has been a benefit, that benefit, as we will show below, has come at too high a price.

It is also clear that U.S. global corporations, in their normal pursuit of profits, are strongly aiding these developments. Therefore it is time to realize *that the interests of our global corporations and the interests of our country have diverged.*

Without a major departure from current U.S. government policies, we can expect that that divergence too will continue. . . .

Confusion Over Free Trade

There is a strong and pervasive belief, especially among many of the most educated and influential, that free trade benefits everyone; that when you lose manufacturing, it is because your comparative advantage is somewhere else, and that it benefits everyone to allow market forces to shift you in the direction of your comparative advantage rather than struggle to keep what you once had.

As your trading partner moves from a less developed to a more developed state . . . , [this] development becomes harmful to your country.

This view represents a fundamental confusion. In most standard economic models countries have fixed capabilities. In this situation market forces will sort themselves out in the way described and the free market free trade result is beneficial. Unfortunately that does not answer or even address the question we are interested in: we are interested in the effect of changes.

What is the effect when a trading partner, in this discussion China, does not hold its capabilities fixed, but rather improves them? Let me state clearly here that economic theory does not say that when your trading partner improves its capabilities, and then market forces act on these new capabilities, that the new free trade result is better for your country than where you were before the change. In fact it can be harmful.

China's approach to trade cannot be described as free trade. It is traditional mercantilism.

What standard models involving change do show, and this is the work that Professor [William J.] Baumol and I have been engaged in for many years, is this: That the initial development of your trading partner is good for you, but as your trading partner moves from a less developed to a more developed state, things turn around. Their further development becomes harmful to your country. Its impact is to decrease your GDP [gross domestic product, a measure of a country's total economic output].

And this result takes into account all the effects. It includes the benefit to consumers of cheaper goods from the newly developed partner (in this case China) as well as the negative impact of losing productive industries in the home country (USA).

Consequently we cannot take refuge, as many do, in simply asserting, in spite of the evidence before their eyes, that China's development is good for the U.S. In fact it is more reasonable to say that theory expects it to have a negative impact with further economic development, and it is further development that is being discussed here.

China's Form of Mercantilism

China's approach to trade cannot be described as free trade. It is traditional mercantilism, a pattern of government policies aimed at advancing Chinese industries in world trade, an approach that has many precedents.

The effect of mispriced currency, subsidies, and the rapid appropriation of foreign know-how allows many Chinese industries to appear on the world scene with prices and capabilities that would have taken decades (if ever) to attain without the aid of these practices. Professor [Willy C.] Shih, who is testifying here today, has well described the destructive effect of these efforts on American industries in some of his writings.

The major emerging economies are becoming more competitive in areas in which the U.S. economy has historically been dominant.

A More Detailed Description

If we look more closely at the development of China we can see what U.S. corporations contribute. We see U.S. corporations, either alone or in joint enterprises with Chinese corporations, building plants in China that enhance both that country's productive abilities and its technical know how. We have seen the goods imported from these enterprises contribute largely to the enormous imbalance of trade since these imports are not balanced by a sufficient counter-flow of exports from this country. We see that today this has resulted in 2 to 3 trillion dollars at the disposal of the Chinese government for the purchase of more treasury notes etc. as in the past, or, as is more likely in the future, for the acquisition of companies and their technology.

In addition, we see U.S. corporations increasingly locating their research and development in China. This is a further and very direct way for China to acquire the necessary know how.

The Consequences

While many economists have been slow to realize that all is not well, we now have this from the Nobel Prize winning economist Michael Spence writing in a widely noticed paper:

> "Until about a decade ago, the effects of globalization on the distribution of wealth and jobs were largely benign. . . . Imported goods became cheaper as emerging markets engaged with the global economy, benefiting consumers in both developed and developing countries.

> But as the developing countries became larger and richer . . . , they moved up the value-added chain. Now, developing countries increasingly produce the kind of high-value-added components that 30 years ago were the exclusive purview of advanced economies.

> The major emerging economies are becoming more competitive in areas in which the U.S. economy has historically been dominant, such as the design and manufacture of semiconductors, pharmaceuticals, and information technology services.

> At the same time, many job opportunities in the United States are shifting away from the sectors that are experiencing the most growth and to those that are experiencing less. The result is growing disparities in income and employment across the U.S. economy. . . . The U.S. government must urgently develop a long-term policy to address these distributional effects and their structural underpinnings and restore competitiveness and growth to the U.S. economy."

Professor Spence reached these conclusions from a careful analysis of government statistics.

With this type of analysis of statistics as well as theory and the evidence of our own eyes, why do things continue unchanged? To see why we must look at the motivation of the American corporation.

Why Corporations Choose China

We might wonder why U.S. corporations are playing such a strong role in the development of China when that it is likely to have a negative impact on the U.S. However this is a direct outcome of the present dominant beliefs of the two countries.

The Chinese government, as their five-year plan shows, is focused on having in their country the leadership of most major and growing industries. In the U.S. in contrast the dominant ideology is laissez-faire [hands-off]: there is a faith that the U.S. corporations, venture capitalists, etc. if left alone, will through the pursuit of profit create the greatest GDP for the country.

Such a complete hands-off policy was not in fact the belief in the earliest days of this country. Initially the mercantilist policies of Britain aimed to keep the colonies as suppliers of natural products while manufacturing and shipping were to the greatest extent possible reserved to the British. After the Revolutionary War, however, Alexander Hamilton urged, eventually successfully, the adoption of protectionist measures to shelter the start of manufacturing in the newly formed independent country.

There have been other periods of protectionism in our history, but most of the time the natural protection of great distance and poor transport has been enough.

Today, with container ships and optical fibers, we are in an entirely different world. Today a global corporation can maximize its profits by sourcing its products or services wherever they can be obtained the cheapest, and sell them wherever the demand is greatest.

The Chinese government, as Singapore's had done earlier, makes intelligent use of this motivation. Through direct subsidies, abated taxes, and mispriced currency they can supplement cheap labor to the point where China becomes the most profitable place to locate the industries China is interested in. China is also able to add to this the lure of a giant growing market and to make, in practice, technology transfer a condition for market entry.

Our corporations, aiming to maximize profit and shareholder value, only hesitate at the thought that the companies they are helping to found might become their future competitors. But in the end it is not surprising that corporate leadership finds the bird in the hand superior to the two in the bush, since profits are reported quarterly, not every five years. Our present executive compensation policies for executives, strongly tied to stock price, then strongly reward these decisions.

The interests of our global corporations have diverged from the interests of our country.

Nor is there any strong reason for our corporations to believe that they are harming their country. Our own government, ignoring in practice Chinese mercantilist policies, has clearly supported the notion of free trade and has even in its official pronouncements supported the idea that outsourcing is good for the country.

Even the rapid decline of the manufacturing sector, which makes up a large part of international trade, has, until very recently, not caused many cracks in the wall of opinion and self-interest that protects the laissez faire status quo.

I want to make clear that our corporations themselves are neither greedy nor evil, though there are people who ascribe our problems to these qualities. In fact they are simply pursuing the widely accepted mandate of maximizing profitability.

They are playing the game by the rules of the game. But in this game, as it is presently constituted, *the interests of our global corporations have diverged from the interests of our country.* . . .

No Royal Road to Prosperity

We need to get used to the idea that there is no effortless road to prosperity. To prosper a country needs to make a range of good products and services, and then keep after them year after year, constantly learning, and improving their capabilities to stay with or ahead of competition. Many products and services of this sort are dismissed as "old hat" or even as "commodities" but many things we consume are of this type. Even commodities can be products or services of high value add per person. They may not be immensely profitable, but profits are not the only thing. High value areas with average profit can contribute strongly to wages and to a widely distributed GDP. And maintaining technical capabilities in competitive areas allows entry into new industries as the technology advances and finds new uses and starts new industries. . . .

We need to consider a U.S. national economic strategy that includes incentives for companies to have high value-added jobs in the United States.

I will not discuss here the usual suggestions about better education and more R&D [research and development]. Proposals of this sort about education and R&D can be helpful. They can only be harmful if they create the mistaken belief that these measures alone can deal with the problem.

The main thrust of this testimony, however, points to the divergence of company goals, focused almost exclusively on profit, and the broader goals of greater GDP and less inequality in the United States. Therefore, we need to turn our attention not only to the familiar suggestions I have just listed, but also to the issue of better aligning corporate and national goals.

Aligning Country and Company

We need to consider a U.S. national economic strategy that includes incentives for companies to have high value-added jobs in the United States. If we want high value-added jobs, let us reward our companies for producing such jobs— whether they do that through R&D and advanced technology, or by just plain American ingenuity applied in any setting whatsoever.

The Asian countries have attracted companies by individual deals with individual companies. We do not have either the tradition or the knowledge or the inclination in the U.S. government to do that. An approach that is better suited to what the United States can do is to use the corporate income tax. We have already used the corporate income tax to spur R&D, so let us use it to directly reward what we are aiming at: High value-added jobs.

Balanced trade is necessary if we are to control our own economic destiny. Without it China or other countries can simply pick the productive industries they want to have as their own . . . and take them over.

One way to do this is to give a corporate tax deduction proportioned to the value added created in the U.S. by a company. Consider two equal size companies, one chooses to send half its work overseas: the other keeps the work in the U.S. The second company will receive double the deduction on its income tax that the offshoring one receives. The effect can be made as strong or as weak as is desired.

Clearly this is only one possibility, if we think in this direction we will find many others.

Balancing Trade—Controlling Our Own Destiny

If the imbalance of trade continues there is nothing to stop the current trend of transferring ever more wealth and power to foreign governments to balance the import of underpriced foreign goods. On the other hand, if trade is balanced, the value of goods imported is matched to the value of goods exported from the country: and those goods and services are provided by jobs in the U.S.

Balanced trade is necessary if we are to control our own economic destiny. Without it China or other countries can simply pick the productive industries they want to have as their own ... and take them over through the usual mercantilist tactics of subsidies, special tax concessions, etc. while accumulating the resulting flow of currency for future use.

What the trade model alluded to earlier also shows is that the ideal position for a country is in fact to be the producer in the most productive industries, while leaving a certain proportion of others to its trading partner. This provides a high standard of living for the country that succeeds in doing this and a much lower one for its trading partner. At present China is the country headed in that dominating direction with its five-year plan, and we are the candidate to be the poorer trading partner with our laissez faire policies. This outcome can be avoided if we prevent these takeovers and keep a substantial proportion of productive activities for ourselves. But this requires balanced trade.

There is of course a litany of approaches to balancing trade ranging from jawboning to tariffs. Tariffs are often dismissed out of hand by economists because of the possibility of retaliatory tariffs from other countries. I only observe here that the approach well described by Warren Buffet has the remarkable attribute that, if adopted by others as a retaliatory measure, the result is not the destruction of trade, but only balanced trade.

Balanced trade is essential, it can be attained, but at present it is not a recognized goal of either Congress or the Administration.

Departing from the Status Quo

Changing the direction we are now headed in will be difficult. Wealthy and powerful segments of our society benefit from the status quo and that includes the leadership of our major corporations, much of Wall Street and many others to whom both the Federal legislature and the Administration turn for advice and political contributions.

To deal successfully with the effect on this country of the rapid industrialization of China, our government needs to take steps to better align the goals of our corporations with the aspirations of our people.

In a globalizing world where nations such as China advance their national interests with well thought out mercantilist policies, it becomes essential to balance trade if we are to control our own destiny. This too calls for new government policies.

The US Trade Deficit Is the Biggest Threat to America's Future

Alec Feinberg

Alec Feinberg is the founder of CitizensForEqualTrade.org, a website that argues that trade deficits are unconstitutional. He is also the author of the 2009 book Truth of the Modern Recession.

Warren Buffett has been quoted as saying, "The U.S trade deficit is a bigger threat to the domestic economy than either the federal budget deficit or consumer debt and could lead to political turmoil . . .". No economic issue today is more pressing than the U.S. trade deficit. This predicament should be America's top priority. It is also a key reason why we have high unemployment. Yet most people in America do not understand this silent killer or what they can do about it. Even most economists are very defensive of our free trade policy, yet none of them can defend free trade's 1000 pound gorilla in the room: the U.S. yearly trade deficit. . . .

The Trade Deficit Threatens the U.S. Economy

Here are important key facts on why the trade deficit now threatens our future:

1. First and foremost, there is absolutely no history that shows that any country including the U.S. can long sustain large yearly trade deficits without putting its future at risk. However, there are instances where empires have

fallen due to trade deficit failures including the 17th century Spanish economy and a trade deficit was partially responsible for the fall of the great Roman Empire.

2. In the last 10 years the trade deficit has averaged $0.55 trillion. The U.S. trade deficit since 1971 is over $7.5 trillion and $6.5 trillion in just the last 20 years. By comparison, the national debt is now about $13 trillion.

3. This year [2010] the current trade deficit through May is $0.170 trillion on track for about $0.4 trillion. It's only lower than average due to the lingering modern recession. The NAFTA [North Atlantic Free Trade Agreement] (from 1993 through 2003) displaced a reported 879,280 jobs. Since the entrance of China, the U.S. has lost another 2.4 million jobs. The two combine for about 3.5 million total jobs lost due to the free trade policy allowing for these large deficits. This number is growing as more and more outsourcing is occurring. Last year [2009] 60% of the U.S. trade deficit was with China.

4. The free trade deficit profits have allowed foreigners to buy up America. According to the Grant Thornton report, "total assets at foreign-owned companies increased 15% to $9.2 trillion in 2005 from $8.0 trillion a year earlier and was more than three times the 1996 total of $3 trillion. Foreign-owned assets totaled just $37 billion in 1971".

5. Foreign-owned companies in the United States have a work force of about 5.3 million, or some 3.5% of all workers. According to the last note (2005), they owned 15% of all U.S. businesses but only employ 3.5% of the workforce. Extrapolating this to 100% ownership (that we are on a crash course for) this would only equate to 25% employment in the U.S. This is our future.

6. Most of the U.S. trade deficit is with China and their ownership is the largest share of U.S. businesses and debt. Thus the U.S. is slowly being sold mostly to China from trade deficit profits dollars obtained from U.S. consumers.

7. The U.S. has a national debt crisis of about $13 trillion. However with the massive trade deficit job losses, this author estimates lost tax revenues of about $1 trillion dollars. Thus the trade deficit contributes significantly to our national debt. Free trade is really not free!

8. We have a viscious cycle, we outsource jobs, increase unemployment, this creates tax losses, the U.S. goes further into debt from these lost tax revenues, the U.S. must then sell more treasury bonds to China and foreigners, consumers are forced to purchase more and more foreign imports with few U.S. made alternative products, this enables [foreigners] to make huge trade deficit profits, which allows them to purchase more U.S. businesses and debt, foreign owned business pay far less taxes then U.S. equivalent businesses and hire fewer American employers, this creates higher unemployment and more tax losses, and the cycle continues.

9. Economic global greed is excessive; the U.S. free trade policy encourages foreigners to cheat as every country wants a piece of America. Well known are unethical trade deficit problems related to: currency manipulation by U.S. trading partners, excessive job outsourcing by U.S. businesses, product subsidies by foreign governments, unfair non-tariff trade barriers by our trading partners, lack of intellectual property rights protection, and product counterfeiting.

10. Because of these massive trade deficit tax losses, this is like a reverse tariff that U.S. citizens must pay on trade

deficit goods. These lost revenues cause increase tax programs. Every citizen must pay more taxes which means in part we are actually supporting all the un-ethical foreign greed issues cited above.

Finally the U.S. trade deficit is not just unethical, it is un-constitutional.

The US-China Trade Imbalance Benefits the United States

US-China Media Brief

US-China Media Brief is a program housed at the University of California Los Angeles Asian American Studies Center and dedicated to creating and promoting a more balanced understanding of the relationship between the United States and China.

Since 1784 when the first American cargo ship the *Empress of China* set sail for Canton with a shipment of ginseng, trade between the United States and China has waxed and waned, except for 22 years between 1949 and 1972 when there was no trade between the U.S. and Mao's Communist China. Since economic reforms in late 1970s, China's share of global trade has grown tenfold.

The U.S. has had a bilateral trade deficit with China since the late 1980s; annual deficits increased throughout the 1990s, and skyrocketed in the first half of the 21st century. At the beginning of 2008, America and China are each other's second largest trading partner, while China has replaced Canada as the largest exporter to the U.S (China is America's third largest export market). In 2007, the United States sent $65.2 billion worth of exports to China, and imported $321.5 billion worth of goods, running up a trade deficit of $256.3 billion, the U.S.'s largest trade deficit ever with a single country. U.S. lawmakers have threatened to slap tariffs and import duties on Chinese goods if China does not reduce its huge trade surplus with the U.S.

"US-China Trade Imbalance," *US-China Media Brief*, UCLA Asian American Studies Center, June 4, 2011. www.aasc.ucla.edu/uschina/trade_tradeimbalance.shtml. Reproduced by permisssion.

What accounts for the huge U.S.-China trade imbalance? Some of the most commonly cited explanations by critics include: i) China restricts access to its markets while aggressively supporting exports by its domestic firms; ii) China's low-wage/low-cost advantage; iii) China's artificially undervalued currency.

The huge number of U.S. imports from China are in labor-intensive products (toys, apparel, shoes, furniture)—industries that have largely moved outside of the U.S. for many years now.

Does China Have Import Tariffs and Quotas That Restrict Access to Chinese Markets?

Although China did impose quotas and licensing requirements on many goods when it first opened itself to world trade in the 1980s, the Chinese government had, by 2005, eliminated most import quotas, as per the terms of accession to the World Trade Organization (WTO) in 2001. A handful of agricultural products were exempt until 2007. And although China still has some import tariffs, they are relatively low and import tariff exemptions are widespread. Figures indicate the effective tariff protection provided to domestic firms in China is among the lowest of any developing country. The accusation that China is restricting its markets to the U.S. is belied by the fact that U.S. exports to China rose 300% between 2000 and 2007, and nearly every U.S. state has recorded triple-digit growth in exports to China since 2000.

Is China's Low Wage-Advantage Responsible for Its Enormous Trade Surplus with the U.S.?

China's low-wage advantage does provide some advantage in international trade, but ... the huge number of U.S. imports from China are in labor-intensive products (toys, apparel, shoes, furniture)—industries that have largely moved outside of the U.S. for many years now. While China imports are only 7.5% of American spending on all consumer goods, they constitute 80% of toys, 85% of footwear and 40% of clothing that Americans buy. It is therefore not a question of Chinese exports beating out U.S. exports of the same goods. On a macro level, there is not too much overlap between Chinese and American production. . . . If anything the U.S. exports to China of skill- and capital-intensive goods such as semiconductors and microprocessors, aircraft, machinery, and petroleum and iron-ore has the effect of raising the relative wages of skilled labor in the U.S. In the end, we are almost talking about apples and oranges here. It's just that we buy more of their apples than they buy of our oranges.

Many of China's exports are actually produced by foreign-invested firms in China, among them many American companies, who then ship these products back to the U.S. for sale.

Is China's Undervalued Currency Responsible for the Huge Trade Imbalance?

Because an undervalued *yuan* [China's currency] makes China exports cheaper and American exports more expensive, most experts agree that some currency revaluation may lead to some decrease in the U.S.-China trade imbalance, but not by nearly as much as most people anticipate. It also may not reduce the U.S.' global trade deficit. Some experts like Michael Pettis, professor at Peking University's Guanghua School of Management, believe that China's currency does affect the trade balance, not so much because of the impact of a stronger yuan on foreign demand for Chinese goods, but rather because of its impact on Chinese domestic monetary policy. . . .

Factors Driving the U.S.-China Trade Imbalance

Americans Consuming, Not Saving: The U.S. has a large trade deficit not only with China but with much of the world. Simply put, this is because the U.S. imports much more than it exports and has done so for many years now. But since 2000 when the U.S. government relaxed its monetary policy to fight recession, the U.S. has been on an especially long-running spending spree, leading to a ballooning in imports. Aided by a long housing boom, Americans borrowed against their rising property values and consumed much more than they were saving. Consumer spending makes up two-thirds of the U.S. economy. The U.S. demand for goods meshed perfectly with China's exports of labor-intensive consumer and household goods.

Relocation of Exports to China from Elsewhere in Asia: Because of the way exports are calculated based on the final place of assembly and export, China, which has become the final assembly point for a number of products such as computers and other electronic items—the component parts of which are produced in other Asian countries—has absorbed the exports previously credited to countries such as Japan, Taiwan and Hong Kong. In fact, China's share of the overall U.S. trade deficit rose from 27% in 1997 to 28% in 2006 while the share of the rest of East Asia fell from 43% to 17% in the same period. This shows that Americans may be importing more from China, but they are now importing less from other Asian nations.

Overcounting China Exports: Many of China's exports are actually produced by foreign-invested firms in China, among them many American companies, who then ship these products back to the U.S. for sale. In fact, in recent years, the majority of China's exports, nearly 60% by value, have been produced by foreign-invested enterprise but have been counted as Chinese exports, thus helping to drive up China's export figures, even though the reality is that U.S. firms are selling to U.S. consumers. For example, Apple's iPod is conceived, patented, and designed in the U.S., but is assembled in China by a Taiwanese firm using component parts from different parts of the world. China, however, only receives $3.70 from the wholesale price of $224. Most of the profits flow back to Apple even though the item is labeled "Made in China" and gets counted as a Chinese export. Typically, about 20% of revenues from each mobile phone, and 30% from each computer made in China are returned to the original investors or patent owners in the U.S. and other countries.

Undercounting U.S. Sales: Conversely, due to the same method of calculating exports, the sale of goods and service to the Chinese by U.S. foreign affiliates operating in China are not counted as U.S. exports to China. This figure totaled $86.5 billion in 2005 (latest available) and was 70% larger than U.S. exports in the same year. If these figures were counted as U.S. "exports", then the total amount of U.S. sales to China would look quite different and the trade imbalance would not be quite so large. Thus are the U.S.-exports side of the numbers in this bilateral trade relationship somewhat misleading and not reflective of the actual balance of commerce. If anything, the primary means by which U.S. firms sell goods [and] services in China is via their foreign affiliates and not via exports, but this is almost never accounted for in the trade debate. Until a better more nuanced method of calculating becomes available, American politicians and citizens alike will have the opportunity to continue to use these somewhat inaccurate numbers to suit their own political ends.

Who Has Benefited from China's Big Trade Surplus with the U.S.?

Certain American Companies: American companies and businesses, especially large firms who have been able to relocate or outsource to China, have been the big beneficiaries as they've seen their comparative costs reduced. In fact, U.S. firms have profited handsomely from their businesses in China with over $4 billion in profits in 2007, 50% more than a year ago. These companies are also the ones most likely to lobby Congress against passing tariffs.

American Consumer: The average American consumer has benefited from the huge volume and wider variety of lower-cost goods (for everything from toys to clothing, footwear and electronics) coming out of China.

American Government: The American government has also benefited from China's trade surplus as China has recycled its foreign exchange surplus into U.S. Treasury securities, which have helped fund everything from America's wars to the bailout of the U.S. sub-prime mortgage crises.

Why Are Critics Still Blaming China for the Huge Trade Imbalance with the U.S.?

Displaced American Workers: Because there is one big and politically powerful group of Americans that have been negatively impacted in China's trade surplus: American workers who have lost their jobs as a direct result of American companies relocating or outsourcing to China. The United States has lost 3.4 million manufacturing jobs since 1998, of which the AFL-CIO estimates about 1.3 million were tied to China. While many economists believe that on balance the low-cost of Chinese-made goods outweighs the loss of American manufacturing jobs, the difficulty is that the benefits of outsourcing (cheaper goods) are more widely distributed, while the negative toll, which although very real for those out of work, is more sector and region-specific, and tends to affect select groups of U.S. workers. These workers can often and do form a strong political bloc to apply pressure on politicians, or are often in "swing states" such as Pennsylvania, Michigan and Ohio that are important to politicians' electoral success. For these displaced workers and politicians, blaming China can be easier than blaming the companies that chose to move their operations to China, and from whom they may be buying cheap goods from at the same time!

Easier than Addressing Domestic Problems: For politicians, blaming China, with its large trade surplus and consistently high growth rates around 10% a year, is easier to do than to address the underlying systemic causes for job loss and to look for ways in which the United States might be more competitive. For example, experts fear that America's global competitiveness may already be undermined by the erosion of its education system, especially in the maths and sciences.

For better or worse, China has become the face of globalization, and rightly or wrongly, has become an easy target for many Americans' anxieties.

Chinese Government's Response

Reduced Incentives for Exporters: After years of complaints from the U.S. and other countries about its growing trade surplus, China has removed or reduced tax rebates on hundreds of items for export including toys, clothing, wood, leather and other goods, which is effectively a tax on these exports, making them more expensive. At the same time, the Chinese say that they cannot be blamed for American's voracious appetite for inexpensive goods.

Looking Ahead

Decrease of China Exports: As of mid-2008, as the United States appears be heading into, if it isn't already in, some kind of recession, demand for Chinese exports will likely decrease. In China, a confluence of factors (including high domestic inflation, more stringent labor laws, the scrapping of export tax rebates, and the stronger value of the yuan) has led to an increase in the cost of doing business in China. Whether and how much those rising costs are passed onto American consumers will likely vary as given today's long and complex supply chains, there are a number of places along the way where Chinese manufacturers and/or the American importers/companies can take on more of the financial burden by cutting into their own profit margins in order to maintain market share. Assuming some increased cost is passed on to American consumers, expect the number of exports from China to the U.S. to decrease as recession-hit Americans reduce their consumption, all of which will certainly lead to some reduction in the trade imbalance (assuming U.S. exports to China remains more or less at the same level).

In the end, the only significant way in which the U.S. trade deficit with China, and with the rest of the world, will decrease is if the U.S. consumes less. Americans' low savings rate means that even if the yuan were to rise appreciably, the U.S. trade deficit will just shift to other countries.

The Battle Over Free Trade: It is commonly accepted that most economists, including the many experts cited in these pages, are advocates of free trade. Economists at the Institute for International Economics and the Center for Strategic and International Studies, for example, argue that over the last 60 years, the U.S. economy is "about a $1 trillion per year richer as a result of the expansion of international trade . . . and could gain another $500 billion annually if the world were to move to totally free trade." There would, however, also be losses of around $50 billion per year in the form of lost jobs, and lower wages for some. It is likely that most of these same economists advocating for free trade are highly skilled and will not have to worry about losing their jobs to another economist in China or India. But for the majority of American workers, the pain of job losses is very real. Little wonder, then, that there is much ambivalence in the U.S. about free trade, as is reflected in the fact that major trade legislation in Congress in the last decade has had about equal numbers of supporters and detractors. For better or worse, China has become the face of globalization, and rightly or wrongly, has become an easy target for many Americans' anxieties. Ultimately, politicians need to know that the attitude of Americans towards global trade will depend in large part on the degree to which the U.S. can provide the proper education and (re)training programs to move displaced workers into new jobs that can take advantage of globalization.

Growing Interdependence: American politicians arguing for tariffs on China exports or worse, an outright ban on certain products, will hurt not only American consumers, but also many American businesses with operations in China. This could in turn lead to greater unemployment back home as these same affected American businesses start to lay off workers here. Also hurt will be Americans who may be shareholders in any of these businesses.

The United States Is Still the Top Global Economic Superpower

Mark Trumbull

Mark Trumbull is a staff reporter for the Christian Science Monitor.

President [Barack] Obama's recent [2011] State of the Union speech carried a blunt message: Continued US prosperity depends on figuring out how to stay ahead of other nations that are out to eat America's lunch.

It's a theme that Mr. Obama has continued to hammer over the past week, and he cites China as a prime challenger—a nation that's now home to the world's fastest computer and largest private solar-research site.

When it comes to China, many Americans agree. Some 47 percent now see it as the world's leading economic power, according to a January poll by the Pew Research Center. Only 31 percent chose the United States.

So just how big an economic threat is China? Is this really a "Sputnik moment" for America, as the president said? The challenge to America is real, but it also shouldn't be exaggerated. The notion that China is already No. 1 is flatly wrong, most economists and Asia experts say.

America Still the Top Global Superpower

"It's a gross misperception," says Robert Sutter, a China specialist at Georgetown University. China is "just not a dominant economy."

Measured in dollar value of output, the US economy is still more than twice the size of China's. And because the US population is about one-quarter that of China, this means the typical person in China has a living standard far below US norms.

If you had to pick a global economic superpower, it's still America.

China's manufacturing is also much less efficient, using far more energy than advanced nations do to produce a given product. And more than half of China's foreign trade, Professor Sutter says, is controlled by foreign firms operating there.

The larger story is that the global economy is becoming multipolar rather than dominated by one superpower.

The Largest Economy

All that said, China is undeniably a force to be reckoned with. It appears to be just a matter of time before China does have the largest economy. Unlike the Soviet Union, which sent the Sputnik satellite into space and later saw its economy unravel, China has built its growing might on a blend of shrewd government guidance, home-grown entrepreneurial drive, and partnerships with the outside world.

China's growth rate isn't remarkable compared with that of other East Asian nations. But its huge population makes China more important—and its government has used that marketplace leverage to lure multinational firms and to arrange for the transfer of valuable know-how in joint ventures. That raises the prospect that China may catch up with the developed world faster than anyone expected.

"Those concerns are legitimate," says Matthew Slaughter, a Dartmouth College economist who specializes in trade issues. In many industries, from automobiles to aerospace, China's advance "has surprised business leaders [and US] government leaders."

According to a 2010 United Nations survey, China is the world's most popular destination for multinational corporations' investment in new factories and other facilities, while India and Brazil bumped the US from second place (in 2009) to fourth.

Little wonder that China feels able to push back against the Obama administration in some global forums.

A Multipolar Global Economy

But the rise of places like India and Brazil as investment magnets makes clear that America's competition is not just from China. The larger story is that the global economy is becoming multipolar rather than dominated by one superpower.

"It's a good thing when other countries are developing capabilities and their standards of living are going up," says Gary Pisano, a Harvard Business School expert on technology strategy. It creates new opportunities for the US—new export markets and imports that boost productivity or enhance the quality of life in the US.

Unlike competition between individual companies or sports teams, countries typically reap mutual benefits from trade, Professor Pisano says.

Solutions for America

But some economists worry that other nations' rapid catch-up could come at America's expense, and even Pisano argues that the US needs policies to ensure its prosperity.

Obama sketched his own policy prescriptions in his Jan. 25 speech—a mix of proposals that include research funding, infrastructure support, education efforts, and reforms of taxes and immigration. But while many economists support those ideas, others call for different approaches, such as tougher trade policies with China or a fiscal austerity plan that might make America less beholden to China as a buyer of Treasury debt.

"The solutions are right here at home," says Joseph Quinlan, chief market strategist at US Trust–Bank of America Private Wealth Management.

A central theme of his new book, *The Last Economic Superpower*, is that America can gain by coaxing forward the trend of globalization, and would be greatly harmed if US-China rivalry degenerated into an economic cold war.

The prescriptions that he and others offer in many ways echo those Obama proposed in his address. "The president's got it right, in terms of we need to invest more in the future," Mr. Quinlan says.

Topping Quinlan's list is better education and retraining of less-skilled workers, and grappling with America's dependence on foreign oil (a problem China shares).

The US still has considerable strengths, from its entrepreneurial tradition to a consumer culture that serves as a test bed for honing new products.

Others emphasize the role that government can play by supporting basic research. And although the private sector excels at applied research, Pisano points to the Internet as an example where government-backed investment paid big dividends.

The list from economists and business groups goes on: Improve outdated infrastructure, reform the tax code to make America a more attractive place for multinational firms, welcome more highly trained immigrants.

Even some free-trade conservatives call for a tougher stand to protect US interests against China. Irwin Stelzer, a contributing editor of the *Weekly Standard*, argued recently that the US must keep closer watch on the transfer of technologies that China pushes for. He says a General Electric [GE] joint venture in avionics, which GE claims is nonmilitary, could well help the Chinese advance "the brains" of their military jets.

Despite all its challenges, the US still has considerable strengths, from its entrepreneurial tradition to a consumer culture that serves as a test bed for honing new products. The need, economists say, is to keep building on those strengths, so America remains a magnet for centers of innovation such as Silicon Valley.

Chinese Inflation and Other Changes May Soon Ease the US-China Deficit

Patrick Smith

Patrick Smith is a correspondent, commentator, editor, author, lecturer, and critic who has written primarily for the International Herald Tribune *and the* New Yorker *magazine.*

It looks like China finally is about to take a great leap forward.

Beijing at last recognizes that an overheating economy is threatening to spin out of control and that it has a serious inflation fight on its hands. And there are signals that Beijing is about to start liberalizing the yuan, China's currency.

Significant Adjustments

They may seem like technical adjustments, but they are significant. This is a nation in the midst of a major transformation from a low-wage exporting economy with a weak currency to a higher-wage consuming economy with a stronger currency. The news of new policies came suddenly, but it marks a shift away from a growth strategy now 30 years old.

China will be a bigger market as wages rise and people are paid in a currency worth more against others. A stronger yuan will help dampen inflation and improve the U.S. trade deficit, which was $273 billion last year [2010] (and another record).

At the same time, Chinese goods at Wal-Mart will not be as cheap as we've come to expect—and neither will anything else Chinese consumers want. Making the yuan a convertible currency means it will start to compete credibly against the

Patrick Smith, "The Next China: A Powerful Consumer Society," *The Fiscal Times*, April 22, 2011. www.thefiscaltimes.com. Reproduced by permission.

dollar, especially in the Pacific region; China's appetite for U.S. debt is almost certain to wane as a result.

Who doesn't want to see a nation of 1.3 billion people climb swiftly up the development ladder toward prosperity? This is the enlightened view. One cannot begrudge the Chinese the material progress the West taught them to honor, regardless of its mixed effects on the rest of us.

As measured by our trade imbalances, we have all been captives of the Chinese Communist Party in its determined grip on power.

The Next China

"The producer economy will increasingly need to give way to a consumer society," Stephen S. Roach, the Morgan Stanley economist, said in a speech at Yale last week [April 11, 2011]. "This transition is equally daunting for the rest of us. Just when the world is figuring out how to cope with a strong China, it will now need to come to grips with 'the Next China.'"

Export-led growth, the strategy China has pursued since its reform period began in 1980, was always a flawed proposition. Exports have grown from 35 percent of GDP [gross domestic product] at the start of the reforms to about 80 percent now—a ridiculous proportion. In the meantime, private consumption hit a record low of 35 percent of GDP in 2008.

Maintaining political power and social stability in such an environment meant that Beijing needed annual growth of 7 percent to 8 percent—and a weak currency to produce it. Bouts of inflation and macroeconomic imbalances were more or less baked into the cake.

The growth model China's reformers chose has also produced a miserable social contract: An authoritarian government that measures prosperity not in the consumption of domestic production but in pieces of paper—the foreign reserves China has accumulated, which now approach $4 trillion. As measured by our trade imbalances, we have all been captives of the Chinese Communist Party in its determined grip on power. (How's that for economic interdependence?)

You have to stand back in awe at the speed with which China appears to be changing course.

Given the arrests of prominent artists and dissidents lately, it's clear there are risks to challenging the reigning orthodoxy in Beijing. But shifting gears toward greater domestic consumption and a more even distribution of wealth was the clear subtext in the five-year plan issued last month [March 2011].

Recent reports seem to confirm that the reformists in Beijing are gaining ground. It cannot be coincidental that (1) Beijing announced an annual 5.4 percent rise in inflation at the end of March, the biggest increase since 2008, (2) Beijing swiftly declared tighter reserve requirements for Chinese banks, (3) a Hong Kong monetary official soon hinted that China will ease controls on the flow of yuan in offshore markets, and (4) Singapore let it be known it wants to be a market for yuan trading. This is Beijing choreography at its best.

Inflationary pressures are one target in China's latest moves; those involving the offshore market will also strengthen the currency. The yuan has informally served as a reserve currency in local Southeast Asian markets for several years. But encouraging this role is a considerable leap for a nation accustomed to managing its monetary affairs as closely as China has until now.

You have to stand back in awe at the speed with which China appears to be changing course. A columnist's confession: This one never thought China would move so swiftly to release its grip on the currency. It is a step Japan was expected to take at the height of its "bubble" 20 years ago, but Tokyo flinched. "Chinese time is three to four times faster than normal development time," Stephen Roach said in New Haven last week. "It has accomplished in three decades what has taken most economies easily a century or more."

CHAPTER 4

Should the United States Toughen Its Trade Policy Toward China?

Chapter Preface

Although the United States and China were allies during World War II, the postwar US-China relationship was hostile for many years until the two sides reestablished official relations in the late 1970s. Following this breakthrough, the United States and China began a dialogue that has covered a broad range of issues—including trade relations, cultural exchanges, science and technology agreements, as well as global strategic and political problems. In recent years, China's rise as a world economic power that sells many of its goods to US consumers has made trade relations one of the most important issues in negotiations between the two nations. President Barack Obama has continued these negotiations with China, and the most recent result of those talks is a US-China framework agreement that was signed by the parties in May 2011, when Chinese President Hu Jintao visited the United States.

The rift between China and the United States developed after World War II as a result of the Chinese Civil War. The United States backed the nationalist Republic of China, which lost the war to communist forces under Mao Zedong. In 1949, the People's Republic of China (PRC) was established under communist rule, but it wasn't recognized as a country by the United States, who instead recognized the Republic of China on Taiwan as the legitimate government of mainland China. Relations between the United States and the PRC worsened during the Korean War, when China supported North Korea and the United States supported the South. Chinese and American troops actually fought each other during this conflict.

The formation of communist regimes in both the Soviet Union and China during this post-World War II period led to the Cold War, several decades of political tension and military rivalry in which the United States and the Soviet Union competed to create, respectively, capitalist democracies and communist governments in countries around the world. Both the United States and China had problems with the Soviets, however, and the two nations eventually began to seek closer ties. In 1972, President Richard M. Nixon became the first US president to visit the Chinese mainland, and formal diplomatic relations between the US government and the PRC were finally re-established in 1979.

Following Mao Zedong's death in 1976, there was a struggle for power in the Chinese Communist Party. Deng Xiaoping emerged as the new Chinese leader, and his economic reforms opened up China to world trade. Under Deng Xiaoping, China's embrace of capitalism and free trade transformed China's economy into a global manufacturing center and major exporter. This development, along with the global recession that stemmed from the 2007 US mortgage and financial crisis, has caused recent US-China negotiations to focus more on economics and trade, as well as other noneconomic issues. Following his election in 2008, for example, President Barack Obama continued and broadened the dialogue initiated by President George W. Bush and Chinese President Hu Jintao, but changed its focus somewhat. Now called the US-China Strategic and Economic Dialogue, US-China negotiations during Obama's administration first focused on four areas: the recession, climate change, nuclear proliferation, and global humanitarian crises. In 2009, President Obama visited China to begin this phase of negotiations, and the visit was followed by two rounds of talks, the first one in Washington in July 2009 and the second one in May 2010 in Beijing. A third round of negotiations accompanied a visit by Chinese President Hu to the United States in May 2011—negotiations that resulted in the "Comprehensive Framework for Promoting Strong, Sustainable and Balanced Growth & Economic Cooperation" (the Framework Agreement), an agreement aimed at building a mutually beneficial economic partnership between China and the United States.

More specifically, the US-China Framework Agreement, according to information released by the two governments, seeks to promote sustainable and balanced economic growth, strengthen both sides' financial systems, and improve trade and investment cooperation. To balance and promote economic growth, for example, China pledged to expand Chinese consumption and imports by raising wages and taking other actions, continuing its currency flexibility, and limiting its discrimination against foreign firms, while the United States said it will increase consumer savings and exports and invest in infrastructure and education to strengthen the US economy. Both sides also promised to undertake and continue financial reforms, and they reaffirmed their commitment to global free trade. Finally, the two countries said they will work to resolve trade disputes, including US concerns about shoddy products and patent infringement of US goods, and China's desire for trade of US high-technology products.

Both sides praised the Framework Agreement. US Treasury Secretary Timothy Geithner, for example, said that he hopes it will mean further increases in the value of the Chinese currency—the yuan—and more opportunities for American companies, both those seeking to operate in China and those seeking to export there. However, some members of Congress and other commentators say that US-China negotiations have produced little in the way of real change over the years, and they argue that it is time to get tougher with China. Given the slow economy and high unemployment in the United States, critics argue, China's harmful trade policies—including its currency manipulation, tolerance of Chinese infringements of US patents, and discrimination against American companies—should no longer be tolerated. On October 12, 2011, the US Senate passed a bill squarely directed at China that would impose new duties on products imported from countries whose currencies are artificially undervalued. The authors of the viewpoints included in this chapter address the question of whether the United States should change or toughen its trade policy toward China.

The United States Must Adopt a Harder Line in Its Economic Negotiations with China

Eliza Patterson

Eliza Patterson is an associate researcher at the Centre for International Studies and Research, located in Paris.

Over the past decade the United States trade policy in regards to China has prioritized diplomatic dialogue aimed at maintaining good relations while persuading China to gradually address US economic concerns. I judge this approach a failure. It is time for a change in strategy.

During the most recent meetings of the US-China Strategic and Economic Dialogue (S&ED) the leader of one of the parties called for the establishment of "a clear timetable and road map" for the other party to make requested changes in its economic policies. That leader was not US Treasury Secretary Geithner, but Chinese Vice Premier Wang Qishan, and the requested changes were in US not Chinese policy.

Washington should take advantage of this echo of its own repeated calls for a timeline for policy changes in China to adopt a firmer, less accommodating approach towards China. The US should present a list of its concerns and insist on concrete action on a specified time schedule as the price for the US refraining from filing complaints in the WTO [World Trade Organization], and imposing protectionist legislation. In exchange the US should agree to grant China its two major requests: market economy status and the negotiation of a bilateral investment agreement. Such an approach, as more fully

Eliza Patterson, "US Trade Policy Vis-à-vis China; Time to Push the 'Reset Button,'" Le Kiosque du CERI (Center for International Studies and Research), June 2011. Link: http://www.ceri-sciences-po.org/archive/2011/juin/art_ep.pdf. Reproduced by permission.

discussed below, will require difficult negotiations with both the US business community and the Congress. However, the potential benefits to the US economy, the international trading system and the [Barack] Obama administration are significant. Moreover, Obama is currently uniquely well positioned to undertake the endeavor.

A Patient Approach

The [Bill] Clinton and [George W.] Bush Administrations, despite public discontent, adopted a patient approach towards China, arguing that China was a "necessary partner" and that the most productive means of achieving desired economic changes was "constructive engagement". The US worked assiduously to ensure China's admission into the WTO and subsequently chose to tackle disagreements through dialogue and persuasion. Harsh rhetoric and punitive legislation were avoided on the grounds that they risked triggering a backlash against US commercial interests. What are the results of this strategy of accommodation? A bag full of promises from China but little if any change in the issues of most concern to the United States. China continues to pursue policies that discriminate against foreign firms, its currency, the value of their currency, the RMB [renminbi, also called the yuan] remains artificially low, violations of intellectual property rights continue, its trade surplus with the US continues to grow and China's human rights record has gotten worse.

The corporate sector wants to see concrete changes in China's policies and practices and they want to see them soon.

During the first years of his administration Obama has been disturbingly inattentive to trade policy, prompting many to wonder if he even has one. In regards to China Obama's policy seems to be Bush redux. He reestablished the Bush era

133

Strategic Economic Dialogue (SED) as the Strategic and Economic Dialogue (S&ED), revived the Joint Committee on Commerce and Trade (JCCT) and, as in the past, promised that these "dialogues among equals" would result in mutually beneficial solutions to a broad range of economic issues. His Treasury Secretary replaced Bush's Treasury Secretary as the lead voice on China. [Timothy] Geithner, like [Henry] Paulson, has called on China to let its currency rise but has refused to take the action-triggering step of officially naming China "a currency manipulator". Like Paulson, Geithner has defended China's go-slow approach to improving intellectual property protection, touted every promise Beijing makes to meet its WTO obligations and repeatedly pleaded with Congress not to enact legislation limiting Chinese imports. Not surprisingly the same policies have had the same dismal results.

The Framework Agreement

The latest, just-completed, round of S&ED talks resulted in a new "US-China Comprehensive Framework for Promoting Strong, Sustainable, and Balanced Growth & Economic Cooperation". A US participant (speaking on background because of the sensitivity of the issue), is reported to have described the agreement as little more than a "procedural framework" replete with promises but lacking any timelines for action, let alone enforceable commitments, from either side. Indeed, US Commerce Deputy Assistant Secretary for Asia said the US "would have preferred much more explicit detail in terms of timeline, in terms of coverage, and in terms of implementation" for the Chinese "commitments" to ensure non-discriminatory application of its industrial and innovation policies, bolster intellectual property protection, and facilitate input from foreign business in the development of Chinese business-related regulations. And the US Chamber of Commerce for whom each of these areas is of major concern hailed the Chinese promises but cautioned that evidence of concrete actions would be necessary to sustain confidence in the S&ED process. Similarly, the US Council for International Business said "if implemented" the Chinese commitments would be significant but noted that past promises on these same issues have gone unfulfilled. The Engage China Coalition, made up of seven US financial services trade associations, applauded the inclusion of financial service reform and liberalization in the agreement but underscored that "meaningful progress" would require that China take more "concrete steps" to open its banking, securities, and insurance sectors. In sum the corporate sector wants to see concrete changes in China's policies and practices and they want to see them soon.

If China wants the US to designate it as a "market economy" it must act like one, letting its currency appreciate and limiting government policies favoring domestic over foreign industries.

A New Path

Obama's recent success in Pakistan [the killing of Osama bin Laden on May 2, 2011] won him renewed respect and popularity both at home and abroad as a strong results-oriented leader. As such he is well positioned to push the reset button in relations with China, a move that will inure to his benefit in 2012. As a follow-on to the S&ED talks Obama should meet with leaders of the multinational business to develop a list of priority concerns. Such a list doubtlessly would include the exchange rate, intellectual property protection, the "indigenous innovation policies", which promote Chinese innovators over those from the US particularly in the area of government procurement, subsidization of green industries, export controls on rare earth minerals, bid rigging on government procurement contracts, barriers to foreign investment in telecommunications and financial services, and frequent harassment of China-based US companies. The lists should then be presented to Beijing making it clear that the US is willing to adopt a roadmap for US policy changes as demanded by Chinese authorities but that its configuration will be determined by policy changes in China. No policy changes will be made in the US in advance of concrete actions by China on the listed priority items. If China wants the US to designate it as a "market economy" it must act like one, letting its currency appreciate and limiting government policies favoring domestic over foreign industries. If China wants the US to ease export controls on high-technology products it must offer verifiable assurances regarding their ultimate civilian use. If China wants a bilateral investment treaty with the US ensuring increased access for Chinese investors in the US it must liberalize its own investment regime and provide adequate investor protections. It must also improve governance within its companies and institute regulatory changes to ensure a clear separation between government regulators and the firms they oversee. And if China wants a halt in US criticism of its human rights record it must change that record.

Will such an approach trigger the long-feared backlash to the detriment of US companies and the US economy more broadly? I think not. For too long US policy has been based on the view of China as a necessary partner with the emphasis on the US needing China, needing its large market for US exports, needing access to its cheap labor for US multinationals' global supply chains, needing its credit to support the US deficit. All this is true. Equally true, and seemingly forgotten however, is that the US is a necessary partner for China and that China knows it. There is no doubt that Beijing recognizes the importance to China of an open US market for its exports and investors. It is also clear that Beijing understands that it is in China's own, long-term best interest to meet US requests regarding enhanced intellectual property protection and RMB appreciation.

Great Politics

Adopting a hard line in economic negotiations with China is not only good policy, it is great politics. Historically when it comes to China policy, there have been two camps in the US. On one side are the "dragon slayers" who see China as an unfair, nefarious adversary and favor the use of economic sanctions to force Beijing to adopt US-advocated policies. In opposition are the "panda huggers" who consider China a necessary, useful and sensitive economic partner and advocate a diplomatic, accommodating approach. Although US policy has been dominated by the "Panda huggers" for decades, in recent years the "dragon slayers" have seen their numbers swell. This trend can be expected to escalate as the 2012 election nears. It is a well-known fact that opponents of trade liberalization in the US shift into high gear at election time. Advocating trade liberalization is almost as lethal for an office-seeker as advocating a tax hike. Support for protectionist policies in contrast is certain to win votes.

The political advantages are particularly significant this year and for this president. Barack Obama was elected with the backing of many anti-trade, pro-human rights advocates and he will need their active support again in 2012. These groups are squarely in the "dragon slayer" camp and have been disappointed with the Administration's failure to make good on its promise of "change" in this as in other areas. A reset of US policy towards one demanding results would go a long way towards ensuring their support, as well as that of the business community, in 2012. It is possible that a few members of the business community with thriving Chinese operations will continue to oppose such a change for fear of being the targets of a Chinese backlash. All indications are that they are outnumbered by those who have become frustrated and angry at Chinese intransigence.

The Quid Pro Quo

Admittedly, the proposed quid pro quo [what the United States gives to China in return for what it seeks from China] in the form of enacting certain changes in US laws as requested by the Chinese will meet with resistance. "Dragon slayers" oppose "pandering to pandas". Nevertheless my discussions with numerous members from this group leads me to believe that ultimately they will see the package as a positive evolution in US policy and reward the Administration on election day.

> *A new hard-line US approach to China ... has the potential to benefit the multilateral trading regime.*

More serious is the reaction of the Congress whose approval is essential if US laws are to be altered. While a majority of the Congress, themselves up for election in 2012, can be expected to embrace a tough line towards China some likely will oppose the proposed quid pro quo. Most controversial will be granting China market economy status. US domestic import-competing companies consider the law denying this status and enabling them to easily secure limits on imports of competitive Chinese products essential to their survival. It will be difficult for members of Congress, particularly in an election year, to vote against these constituents. To win their support the Administration will have to do what all Administrations do: bargain. The Executive branch has many favors it can exchange for votes. Federal funds for members' favored infrastructure projects, the president's endorsement of unrelated legislation of importance to members, the president's attendance at a campaign rally are just a few of the possibilities.

At the close of the latest S&ED talks Chinese Vice Premier Wang Qishan said that the most important thing the Obama Administration can do for the US-China relationship is to "depoliticize economic issues with China". One year before a presidential election this is not going to happen and the Obama Administration should make this crystal clear. In fact, this political reality provides the President with additional leverage. Surely Beijing understands the political climate in the United States. By now it has sufficient international negotiating experience to know that the number one rule is to understand the politics and policy formation process of the other side.

Benefits for Multilateral Trade

A new hard-line US approach to China also has the potential to benefit the multilateral trading regime. The latest round of multilateral trade negotiations under the aegis of the WTO—the Doha Development Round—has ground to a halt largely due to disagreements between developing and developed nations in the areas of agriculture and services trade. The divide has come to seem insurmountable as good will has been replaced by anger and frustration on both sides. However, if the major developing and the major developed country—China and the US—focused on working together to find a solution, it is likely one could be found. At least that is the thinking of involved negotiators. Representatives of the US and the EU [European Union] as well as the WTO's Director General have all urged China to become actively involved, to become, in the words of a former US Trade Representative "a responsible stakeholder". However, as long as bilateral disagreements dominate the US-China economic relationship the two countries will not be able to focus on working together in this way. If the new US approach advocated in this paper is successful in bringing about concrete changes in Chinese policies and subsequently in US policies bilateral tensions would ease and the two parties could focus on the more important task of rescuing the multilateral trading system of which both are major beneficiaries. There has been considerable talk over the past half decade of a G2—made up of the US and China—becoming a leading force on a host of global issues. Trade and the WTO would not be a bad place to start.

The United States Must Compete in Its Own Self-Interest

Clyde Prestowitz

Clyde Prestowitz is founder and president of the Economic Strategy Institute, a private, nonprofit public policy research organization that focuses on globalization and related economic issues.

The U.S. has been experiencing an erosion of economic productive power. America's telecommunications infrastructure, critical in an interconnected global economy, now ranks 15th in the world. And in a key emerging industry—clean energy—the U.S. has lost its competitive edge. What's more, because of high business tax rates and a lack of federal incentives for businesses to locate here, the U.S. has become relatively unattractive for investment. In other words, America's wealth-producing capacity has waned. It's not irretrievable, but the hour to do so is getting late.

False U.S. Assumptions About Trade

Why has America's ability to produce wealth declined? Because U.S. lawmakers pursue policies—domestic and international—that are inappropriate for the reality within which we currently live. Our assumptions about how the global economy should work are really shared only by the United Kingdom—not by Germany, not by Japan, and not by China.

As I wrote in *The New Republic*, "What's at issue is a clash between the outdated U.S. orthodoxy of international free markets and the new international reality of strategic global-

Clyde Prestowitz, "America Must Compete to Retrieve Its Lost Prosperity," futureo fuschinatrade.com, accessed September 28, 2011. Copyright © 2010–2011 by futureo fuschinatrade.com. Reproduced by permission.

ization—between, on one hand, embracing free trade and eschewing subsidies, even when other countries do not, and, on the other hand, actively using government to promote jobs and trade."

[It] is not about the U.S. stopping China from being successful.hellip; It is instead about America doing what China has long done—competing, for its own self interest.

Instead of basing its policies on false assumptions, the U.S. must understand the global economic reality and respond to it appropriately. As much as the U.S. implores, neither Germany nor Japan nor China is likely to become like America. So the task for America, then, becomes one of adjustment—of realigning its own policies in light of this economic reality.

For example, China's active currency intervention, which holds the renminbi [the Chinese currency] 15–40 percent under value, keeps the price of the country's exports artificially low. But it also means that China is in effect setting the price not only of Chinese goods and services but also American goods and services, as well as the value of the American dollar. That currency manipulation has certainly been good for China, but it has not been good for the U.S. So America must stand up and act in its own self interest, regain control over the value of the U.S. dollar and the prices of American products.

Competing for U.S. Interests

But this scenario, in which America really begins to compete—this imagination of the future of trade between the U.S. and China—is not about the U.S. stopping China from being successful. It's not a zero-sum contest. It is instead about

America doing what China has long done—competing, for its own self interest. It is about America doing what is good for America.

That means the U.S. focuses on maintaining a high standard of living and opportunity, ensuring a wealth-producing base to maintain the American way of life (which means, in part, high-quality infrastructure and education). It means a social and economic environment within which people can realize that quintessential American dream: that by working hard, they can achieve success.

So what are the ways that America will begin to act in its own self interest? By . . .

- Launching formal talks in the IMF [International Monetary Fund] to address China's currency manipulation.

- Asking the WTO [World Trade Organization] to rule whether China's currency manipulation amounts to an illegal subsidy of exports.

- Calling a G20 [referring to a group of the world's industrialized nations] conference to discuss restructuring the global financial system with an eye to developing policies that would eventually lead to the replacement of the U.S. dollar as the world's predominant international reserve currency (China's Premier Wen Jiabao has also called for such discussions).

- Initiating countervailing duty investigations on a broad range of imported products that benefit from the subsidy of the currency undervaluation.

- Offering attractive federal incentives designed to lure multinational corporations to locate (or remain) here. As I advocated in my piece in *The New Republic,* the Secretary of Commerce should create an Invest in America office, modeled on Singapore's Economic Development Board. Every domestic and foreign business leader visiting the U.S. should hear how important it is to consider investing in America.

- Reducing the corporate tax rate (next to Japan's, it is the world's highest) to 15 percent on profits on new investment in tradeable goods and services—to incentivize the production of Made in the USA goods and services for export.

- Developing high-quality infrastructure that rivals other countries'. I've suggested before that American policy-makers should create a "Rebuild America's Infrastructure" program with an Infrastructure Bank at its core to bring America's infrastructure up to par.

- Creating its own indigenous innovation policies. Today's Manufacturing Czar should become a Competitiveness Czar, responsible for identifying industries in which America could compete and proposing measures (including tax incentives and government contracts) to ensure that those industries flourish.

And what are the ways that China will continue to act in its own self interest? China's economy has grown at more than 9 percent annually on average over the last decade. That compares to a growth rate of about 2 percent or less in the U.S. and other developed economies. Some call China's growth a miracle. But it is actually the result of very deliberate strategic planning. For example:

- Subsidized land, energy, and water; value-added tax (VAT) rebates on exports; tax holidays; outright capital grants; R&D incentives for "strategic" industries.

- China has long said that certain key sectors of the economy will remain "state dominated." Those state-owned companies easily thrive within such protections and are now looking beyond China's borders to compete globally.

- China improves its technological capability (and thus its productivity) by "learning from" foreign companies invested in China.

- In 2009 China proposed "indigenous innovation" regulations that will require government procurement to favor products that include Chinese intellectual property. And the central government has mandated the replacement of foreign technology—chips, software, communications hardware—with Chinese technology in critical infrastructure within a decade.

Then what happens? As the U.S. turns to a strategy of boosting its global economic competitiveness, the relative cost of American exports (compared to other world exports) falls; the volume of U.S. goods and services exported around the world rises; the relative cost of Chinese goods and services (compared to U.S. goods and services) rises; and the volume of Chinese goods and services imported into the U.S. falls (as the U.S. satisfies domestic demand with more Made In the USA products).

Compared to the status quo, then—China doing mercantilist policies and the U.S. doing nothing—China must focus on growth led by rising domestic demand rather than by exports. If China does that, its economy can continue to develop and the Chinese can continue to get rich just as quickly as they are now. In the U.S., the economy's wealth-producing capacity endures, and American per capita income continues to rise by about 2% (real trend) a year.

The United States Should Crack Down on China's Currency Manipulation

Dustin Ensinger

Dustin Ensinger is a contributing blogger for Economy in Crisis, a website dedicated to educating the public about the decline of the US industrial base.

China may very well be the worst protectionist country in the history of the world, according to one economist.

Fred Bergsten, president of the Peterson Institute for International Economics, also served in the White House and Treasury Department. He told *Reuters* that China's currency manipulation may give it the title of the world's worst protectionist.

"China has intervened massively in the foreign exchange markets for at least five years, buying at least $1 billion every day to keep the dollar strong and its own renminbi weak," he said.

"This is by far the largest protectionist measure adopted by any country since the Second World War—and probably in all of history."

Distorted Trade Hurts U.S. Jobs

China's currency is estimated to be undervalued by as much as 40 percent. It acts as both an export subsidy for domestic manufacturers and an import tariff for foreign competitors looking to sell goods and services in the enormous Chinese market.

Dustin Ensinger, "China: Worst Protectionist Ever?," Economyincrisis.org, September 6, 2011. Reproduced by permission.

The distorted trade not only gives Chinese companies a major advantage over its competitors, it also affects Americans' jobs.

Since entering the WTO [World Trade Organization] in 2001, trade with China has resulted in the loss of 2.3 million jobs through 2007, according to the Economic Policy Institute. In 2006 alone, the trade gap with China resulted in the loss of 366,000 American jobs.

Fighting Currency Manipulation by China

Numerous lawmakers have introduced legislation that would allow the U.S. to implement measures that would counteract Chinese currency manipulation. However, none of those measures have passed both houses of Congress.

The Treasury Department could unilaterally decide to punish China for purposely undervaluing its currency. Twice a year, it releases a report on different currencies around the world. Each time it has released the report, it has failed to label China as a currency manipulator, which would then allow the U.S. to automatically impose countervailing duties on China's imports.

Alternatively, the U.S. could take the case to the WTO and argue that China's undervalued currency acts as a de-facto export subsidy, which is illegal under the organization's rules.

If the U.S. fails to act, either legislatively or administratively, China will continue to post massive trade surpluses with the U.S., take American jobs and factories and build up a massive war chest of dollars that can be used to gain leverage in Washington politics.

The United States Should Prevent China from Buying US Debt

Peter Navarro and Greg Autry

Peter Navarro is a business professor at the University of California at Irvine, as well as a CNBC contributor and the coauthor, with Greg Autry, of the 2011 book Death by China: Confronting the Dragon—A Global Call to Action. *Greg Autry also teaches macro economics at UC Irvine.*

The Currency Exchange Rate Oversight Reform Act, informally known as the Currency Bill, received a great deal of attention in the media a few weeks back [October 2011]. Passed by the Senate, the bill was a solid piece of legislation aimed squarely at the most destructive of China's many abusive trade policies. However, despite considerable support, the House isn't taking it up and there is no reason to expect President [Barack] Obama to sign it or for his administration enforce it.

This is because, much of our government, including this White House, has been co-opted by the multinational corporations that profit from China's trade abuses and exploitation of its labor and environment. This cozy system drives up returns on U.S. capital invested in China, making the rich richer, while it undermines the value of American labor, making the poor poorer. No amount of U.S. government largesse can overcome this structural problem.

What is needed to fix our economic problem at home is a show of American resolve on trade. China's pushing its Yuan up dramatically the day before the Senate vote clearly demon-

Peter Navarro and Greg Autry, "Think Different About Chinese Currency Manipulation," *The Huffington Post*, November 17, 2011. Reproduced by permission.

strated what every Chinese dissident will tell you: the Boys from Beijing [China's capital city] respect power and action, not supplication.

That hasn'st stopped China's apologists in America from rushing to the barricades in defense of the abomination they call "free trade," a one-sided wealth transfer mechanism that has transformed America's manufacturing heartland into a wasteland and Shanghai into a towering dreamscape. Republican Senator Bob Corker of Tennessee trotted out the usual scare tactics and howled that the bill's sanctions would launch a "trade war." Well, Senator, 25 years of escalating trade deficits looks an awful lot like a trade war from Cleveland or Detroit.

[China's] funding America's debt keeps stimulus addicts like our President quietly inside China's pocket and also supplies China with a financial "nuclear option" against America.

Cut Chinese Purchases of U.S. Debt

However, for those who can't stomach a tariff or a sanction under any guise, we need an outside the box proposal, presidential candidate Buddy Roemer and [Greg Autry] offer an elegantly simple suggestion: disable China's currency manipulation mechanism now, and simultaneously defuse its growing threat to our national sovereignty.

To keep its currency trading within a specified range, China runs a "sterilization process." This involves vacuuming a vast amount of our Wal-Mart dollars out of their ever-growing trade surplus. The Chinese must ensure that these dollars are not eventually sold on the foreign exchange markets because that would drive down the relative price of the U.S. currency, making American goods more competitive in Chinese and global markets—the one thing our so-called "trading partner" never wants to happen. So, China buys U.S. Treasuries as the surest way to make these greenbacks "go away," and as has become the largest holder of U.S. treasury securities, to the tune of $1.1 trillion or nearly 25 percent of total foreign holdings. By comparison, the second largest holder is Japan, at $936 billion, followed by the United Kingdom at $397 billion.

Clearly, borrowing money from China in order to buy their stuff has never been an effective fiscal or economic plan for America.

Beijing's funding America's debt keeps stimulus addicts like our President quietly inside China's pocket and also supplies China with a financial "nuclear option" against America. A recent *People's Daily* article titled "China must punish U.S. for Taiwan arm sales with 'financial weapon'" urges Beijing to establish a "direct link between the U.S. Treasury bond purchase and U.S. domestic politics." Let's be clear, *People's Daily* editorials do not reflect individual opinions, but are actually subtle announcements of new Communist Party doctrine. Do any of us, even "free trade" loving Senators, wish to live in an America where the Chinese Communist Party dictates our politics?

We should address this clear and present danger to our economy and our sovereignty straight on and cut off Beijing's purchases of American debt. Shutting off China's access to this currency disposal site will break their sterilization system. We could and should prevent any hostile nation from buying or redeeming our bonds; Congress and the President should pass special legislation that directs the Treasury not to accept bids on new U.S. bond issues from China. If China threatens to "dump" U.S. debt, we should declare the serialized bonds they hold to be "non-transferable." They could, of course, buy our debt on the secondary market, but the dollars they used would hit the foreign exchange market—precisely what they were trying to prevent in buying them to begin with.

Yes, we hear those howls of, "how will we finance our deficit?" Clearly, borrowing money from China in order to buy their stuff has never been an effective fiscal or economic plan for America. Lowering our trade deficit would raise GDP [gross domestic product, a measure of a country's total economic output], increase government revenues and plug a giant leakage that renders any Keynesian [a school of economic thought based on the concepts of economist John Maynard Keynes] stimulus ineffective. In the meantime, we have Americans and real friends who remain ready buyers of our bonds, when they pay sufficient returns.

Yes, removing a source of demand will drive up bond yields and make it harder for the Fed [Federal Reserve] to keep interest rates near zero. So what? Paying higher rates to our kids rather than sending checks to Beijing will close another leakage. Interest rates are not America's problem; jobs are America's problem! Bankers—Roemer has run a bank— really don't want to loan money at four percent for 30 years, and all the new regulatory requirements have made it increasingly difficult to qualify for a loan anyway. Further, Americans are more debt-adverse and businesses see no reason to borrow money for expansion—other than to invest it in China.

In any case, if the current currency bill actually worked and China stopped their sterilization process, their bond purchases would halt! They don't buy those things because they love us or think it's a good investment. They lose money doing it. No matter how we stop the Chinese currency scam, we will need to find a new way to fund our debt, or better yet, the will power to control it.

Blocking Chinese Investments in the United States

Lastly, we need to realize that China's taste for America extends beyond bonds. A China which threatens to influence our domestic politics via bond purchases would not hesitate to leverage a communist-controlled Bank of America or Con-Agra. Therefore, we must also block the Chinese government, its State Owned Enterprises and their proxies from investing in U.S. corporations, land and resources, again preventing them from burying those dollars they don't want to see exchanged on the global markets.

Decades of engagement with China's corrupt and brutal rulers have produced no improvement in that regime and the promise of access to their market remains illusionary. Defense of our economy and our national sovereignty demand that we do something. Keeping the Chinese government from burying their "sterilized" dollars in American soil is the cleanest way to start.

US Policymakers Should Worry About China's Subsidies to State-Owned Chinese Companies

Derek Scissors

Derek Scissors is a research fellow at the Asian Studies Center, part of The Heritage Foundation, a conservative think tank.

There is persistent concern in the U.S. that Chinese currency policy is costing American jobs. The main argument is that jobs are lost because China's currency, the yuan, is weak—it is not worth enough as compared to the dollar, giving Chinese companies an unfair price advantage in international trade.

There is no genuine evidence to support this claim. As shown below, over the past 20 years, U.S. unemployment has been low when the yuan is weak and high when the yuan is strong. It has been so because American, not Chinese, policies determine unemployment levels. The yuan is incidental. Congressional action to punish China for its exchange rate policy, such as that now being considered, will do nothing to create jobs in the U.S.

There are Chinese actions that *do* harm the U.S. These same policies also harm the rest of the world. The most damaging can be grouped under the mantle of subsidies.

A Problem of Chinese Subsidies

The current government in Beijing is utterly committed to state dominance of the economy. To ensure this outcome, it has granted various kinds of subsidies to state-owned and

Derek Scissors, "The Facts About China's Currency, Chinese Subsidies, and American Jobs," *Backgrounder*, no. 2612, The Heritage Foundation, October 4, 2011. Reproduced by permission.

state-controlled enterprises, effectively blocking access to most of the market, among other problems. If China is to become a good economic partner, it must cut these subsidies back.

It is unwise to get into a battle of subsidies with the People's Republic of China.

This is a daunting goal. The first step, however, is clear: The U.S. should identify and measure the extent of Chinese subsidies. This will strengthen the American case in multilateral discussions and any needed decisions by the World Trade Organization (WTO). It will also enable focused proposals in bilateral talks—an important change from the current situation—and a clear measurement of whether progress is being made.

All sides in the China conversation know subsidies are a serious issue. Substantial reductions will take years, not months. But the most important Chinese distortion of global trade can be reduced without breaking trade rules, if the U.S. focuses on what truly matters.

No Competition for State-Owned Enterprises

It is unwise to get into a battle of subsidies with the People's Republic of China (PRC). Beijing has myriad ways to intervene in the market, starting with simply telling companies and banks what to do. The ability to order firms to act, using laws made at the whim of the Communist Party, is the heart of the biggest of Chinese subsidies: protection against competition through tight regulatory control of market entry and exit.

There is a good deal of confusion about what constitutes "state-owned" or "state-controlled" but Chinese regulatory statutes make clear the state's true role. By central government edict, the state must control nearly all major industries. For some—oil and gas, petrochemicals, electric power, and telecommunications—the state must own all the participating firms. In others—aviation, coal, and shipping—the state must control the sector as a whole. In yet others—autos, construction, machinery, metals, and information technology—the state's role is to expand until it controls the sector. State-owned enterprises (SOEs) also control most of insurance, the media, railways, and China's huge tobacco industry. Perhaps most important, nearly all banks are state-owned, providing a huge lever to control the rest of the economy.

Regulatory protection does not only block competition with state-controlled firms, it also contributes heavily to the daunting problem of an unbalanced global economy.

State-Dominated Industries in China

The combined market share of importers, foreign firms based in the PRC, and Chinese private companies is not permitted to expand beyond a certain, often minimal position. There are other examples of regulatory favoritism but there is no greater subsidy than assured market share, in this case of a large market. Further, while SOEs are said to compete with each other, the competition can be difficult to recognize. Under the current government, a huge group of protected SOEs—very large and centrally controlled—and smaller but much more numerous provincial SOEs can never lose a competition because they are never permitted to go bankrupt.

Struggling SOEs are directed entirely by the relevant government arms, with effectively no obligation to creditors or other shareholders. They are typically merged with other SOEs, with no downsizing and thus no market share made available to non-state entities. Indeed, the government now seeks to orchestrate consolidation of weaker SOEs while at the same time driving out non-state firms. This is occurring most famously in rare earths, but also in aluminum, auto, cement, steel, and

155

many larger industries. In all cases, the desired result is a few large firms, all state-owned. This is just one small step short of a state monopoly.

As with a monopoly, barring competitors allows SOEs to raise prices and lower quality. This effectively serves as a tax on Chinese consumers. Because it is a huge subsidy for firms, it also subsidizes investment. The PRC's now infamous imbalance between investment and consumption did not exist before the current Chinese government came to power in late 2002. It arises in large part from regulatory protection discouraging consumption and encouraging investment. Regulatory protection does not only block competition with state-controlled firms, it also contributes heavily to the daunting problem of an unbalanced global economy.

Traditional Subsidies

The second set of subsidies stems from a financial system rigged to boost SOEs. Access to domestic securities markets is heavily biased in their favor. Due to government-controlled interest rates, ordinary depositors now receive less on their savings than they pay in inflation—negative real returns. Banks gain from this low payout but themselves can only charge for borrowing at roughly equal to the rate of inflation. Banks also must place reserves at the central bank, the People's Bank of China, at very low yields, costing revenue.

For its part, the People's Bank faces a rapidly deteriorating balance sheet due to irresponsibly loose monetary policy. Finally, non-state enterprises receive a very small share of loans and often pay exorbitant rates. This is in large part because, unlike SOEs, non-state firms can actually go bankrupt and are therefore seen as riskier.

In contrast to the hardships for all other participants in the credit system, SOEs borrow immense amounts at essentially no cost. The base one-term loan rate is below the rate of inflation, so that the real cost of borrowing is negative for those that qualify, all of which are state-controlled. Bank loans spiked past $1.4 trillion in the 2009 stimulus, another $1.2 trillion in 2010, and $550 billion in the first half of 2011, about 80 percent of which went to SOEs. That is over $2.5 trillion in very low-yield financing in less than 3 years—a result to make even the U.S. government proud. At the level of individual enterprises, the numbers are equally astonishing. Huge loans are made to firms in designated strategic industries but also to firms having financial difficulties.

For nearly two decades, there has been no real connection between the value of the yuan and U.S. unemployment.

The warped financial system is the second force creating the imbalance between investment and consumption. The ability to borrow at no cost drives up investment. The return on saving is negative. Yet people must still save for housing, education, health, and retirement, so savings rates are high and consumption correspondingly limited. Here, too, Chinese subsidies do not just cause massive problems for competing firms, they weaken the global economy.

Land has become a third important subsidy. Land is in principle state-owned, so that acquiring land for expansion is easy and comparatively cheap for most SOEs. The size of this subsidy is growing rapidly because land value in the PRC has soared in the past few years. Acquiring land is, unsurprisingly, difficult and increasingly expensive for non-state companies. These also face the additional problem of insecure ownership rights—provincial governments can evict them from operating sites, sometimes in order to eliminate or reduce competition for their SOEs. Other inputs to production are also subsidized, with privileged access to low-cost power perhaps the most important of these.

Finally, China's currency policy also acts as a subsidy, but not an important one for the U.S. The yuan is pegged to the dollar, so the dollar cannot fall against the yuan at the same speed it has against other currencies. This is what is meant by the yuan being "artificially weak." However, the other currencies are most disadvantage. Since the dollar is falling against most currencies, the yuan has been as well, even though the PRC still runs the world's largest trade surplus. China has gained a competitive advantage against these countries due to the dollar peg, even while the yuan has risen against the dollar itself.

From the American perspective, the yuan's 24 percent rise against the dollar since June 2005 has coincided with a rising bilateral trade deficit, in stark contrast to the predictions of those calling for revaluation. More broadly, for nearly two decades, there has been no real connection between the value of the yuan and U.S. unemployment. This is not a surprise—American unemployment is naturally determined by American policies, not Chinese.

Unfair Competition

China has multiple sources of genuine competitive advantage, but many firms do not profit from these. They are suppressed to ensure the dominance of SOEs, whose advantages are not market-based. When competing in the Chinese or global markets, private Chinese firms, multinationals based in the PRC, and foreign companies in home or third markets face an unbalanced fight.

To illustrate, state giants are powerfully protected in oil and telecom, where the huge Chinese market should draw dozens of competitors. Instead, these are barred. As a result, industry leaders China National Petroleum Corporation (CNPC) and China Mobile reported 2009 profits greater than the 500 largest Chinese private firms combined. There are only two private banks and foreign banks have less than 2 percent of banking assets. The figure is similar for insurance premiums. There are no foreign majority-owned auto companies.

Multinationals may be doing better than domestic private firms but they still cannot share in what are reported to be huge profits in metals or banking. Much-discussed operating and other restrictions on multinationals are all secondary to this simple cordoning-off of most of the market.

Imports are also dramatically impacted. Imports of steel and ships, once important, are now trivial in overall production. The requirement that SOEs, such as First Auto Works, come to control the domestic market has kept auto imports below 5 percent of total sales. A large segment of machinery follows a similar track, and the current target for import displacement in favor of domestic production is information technology.

Rather than wasting still more time, the U.S. should now turn to the true problem with Chinese policy. . . . [It] should identify and measure—and continuously update the measurement—the extent of subsidies.

Guaranteed revenue, domestic production subsidies, and yet more capital subsidies specifically targeted at expansion overseas also make SOEs an increasingly formidable presence outside the PRC. The Heritage Foundation's China Global Investment tracker is the only public dataset on Chinese outward investment besides bonds. Since 2005, this investment exceeds $250 billion, changing China from an afterthought to a direct and growing competitor in South America and Europe. State entities account for more than 90 percent of the spending.

Beijing also selects sectors it considers ripe for commercial opportunity to receive subsidies—such as regulatory protection and capital—that enable Chinese firms to rapidly claim

159

huge shares of the world market. Solar energy is the prime example at the moment, with Chinese production of solar panels soaring but most of the output heading overseas. There have been many others in recent years, including rare earths.

The American Response

The reason the exchange rate receives so much political attention is it appears to be simple, while subsidies do not. The evidence makes clear, however, that there is no reason to expect American job creation from another 25 percent rise in the yuan against the dollar. Policies aimed at compelling the yuan to rise may seem simple, but they will accomplish nothing for the U.S.

Rather than wasting still more time, the U.S. should now turn to the true problem with Chinese policy. As should be expected in a huge economy with many forms of state intervention, Chinese subsidies will not be easy to roll back. The first step is not politically attractive but it is absolutely necessary: The U.S. should identify and measure—and continuously update the measurement—the extent of subsidies.

In this measurement, protection against competition must be included. This will be inexact and therefore controversial. It will also be difficult. However, if regulatory protection is not included, subsidies will be seriously underestimated and considerable harm will continue to be inflicted on American companies and the balance of the global economy. Including regulatory protection along with capital, land, and other subsidies means that initial estimates are likely to be somewhat imprecise. However, with a sustained effort, they will improve over time.

Measuring subsidies will have three uses. The first is within the WTO. The WTO will not fully accept American figures on Chinese subsidies, since some documented transfers will be beyond the scope of WTO rules. However, as measurements improve and become more sophisticated, the germane components will be increasingly accepted in WTO cases. While WTO decisions take a good deal of time to reach and implement, the U.S. can be permitted to counteract Chinese subsidies while the process is under way. In addition, the WTO process can serve as an instrument to induce the PRC to share information on its subsidies.

Second, in the bilateral relationship, America presently approaches China in the Strategic and Economic Dialogue (S&ED) and other forums with numerous, scattered, and ultimately vague demands, which have little chance of ever being met. A comprehensive measurement of subsidies gives the U.S. both the ability to make concrete proposals and, even more important, an objective way to measure progress on those proposals over time. Without this innovation or one similar, bilateral talks will continue to be frustrating, with almost no progress on major issues for a second decade.

And third, if appeals to the WTO are ultimately seen as inadequate and properly conducted bilateral negotiations fail, a measurement of subsidies is necessary to determine the best further response. Barring such evidence, American action could be seen as arbitrary and protectionist, rather than corrective. U.S. actions should therefore include the following:

1. *Congress should not focus on the U.S.-China exchange rate, as this will accomplish nothing positive for the American economy.* Legislation will not bring the results Congress desires.

2. *The United States Trade Representative (USTR),* with assistance as necessary from the Department of the Treasury, International Trade Commission, and Department of Commerce, *should immediately begin the process of measuring the extent of subsidies* provided by Chinese regulatory protection, non-market loans, land grants, and other actions.

3. *The USTR should inform the WTO of any Chinese failure to disclose these subsidies,* as the PRC is required to do by the WTO.

4. *In preparatory talks for the 2012 S&ED, the Department of the Treasury,* with any necessary assistance from the USTR, *should notify the Chinese side that the U.S. will be exclusively discussing subsidies in this round* of the economic side of the dialogue.

First, Assess Subsidies

There is a long-running debate over where the U.S. should focus its efforts on encouraging China to resume market reform of its economy. The debate has caused American policy to be distracted and ineffective and it is past time for it to end. The yuan-dollar exchange rate is not important to the performance of the U.S. economy. Issues such as protection of intellectual property certainly matter but subsidies, when properly defined and understood, are the core problem. They block exports to China, distort imports from China, harm foreign companies operating in China, and unbalance the entire world economy.

What to do first should also be an easy decision. No action will be successful until the U.S. has a reasonable and formalized understanding of the full set of Chinese subsidies, especially protection against competition. The evaluation should start as soon as possible. With that, multilateral and bilateral negotiations at least gain the prospect of being fruitful. If both the PRC and the WTO prove unable or unwilling to act to curb subsidies, the U.S. will then face the truly difficult decision of how best to limit their damaging effects.

The US Government Must Plan for the Threat of Chinese Investment in the United States

Ting Xu

Ting Xu is a senior project manager at the Bertelsmann Foundation, a nonprofit policy organization based in Germany with a North American arm in Washington, DC.

The United States and China have long lobbed verbal grenades across the Pacific, each blaming the other for global imbalances due to currency manipulation or fiscal irresponsibility. But a new challenge to Sino-US relations is emerging, one that will brush aside the bones of contention that now occupy policymakers—Chinese investment in the United States.

So far, Washington hasn't unveiled a clear strategy to address this impending source of friction. It needs one.

China's Foreign Investment Strategy

With $3 trillion in foreign currency reserves, China needs to invest its money abroad. Its domestic, export-led economy is no place to absorb all the capital. In addition, inflation is stubbornly high and rising labour costs have begun to push production elsewhere, threatening China's solid growth rates. Meanwhile, limited investment options have led to an alarming asset bubble.

Beijing must tread a fine line in trying to keep its economy growing at a sustainable pace while developing a model for growth that no longer depends on cheap labor and the abun-

Ting Xu, "The Next Big Threat to US-China Ties," *The Diplomat*, July 13, 2011. Copyright © 2011 The Diplomat. All Rights Reserved. Reproduced by permission.

dant use of natural resources. That means restructuring the Chinese growth model by moving its manufacturing sector up the value chain. Greater investment in the world's advanced, industrialized countries would spur this effort, and that's exactly what the Chinese government is encouraging companies to do. Highest on the list of investment targets is the United States.

Beijing's 2010 Report on China's Economic and Social Development Plan and its 12th Five-Year Plan offer a glimpse of this strategy. The first document showed Chinese non-financial foreign direct investment (FDI) reached $59 billion in 2010, up 36.3 percent from just a year before. The second document unveiled a policy focus on boosting innovation in strategic emerging industries and upgrading traditional industries. Both will require investment in Western leading-edge, high tech sectors. A report by the Asia Society predicts Chinese investment abroad will soar to $1 trillion by 2020, with much of it going to the United States. In another sign of this trend, a recent survey by the China Council for the Promotion of International Trade (CCPIT) pointed to the United States as the most attractive overseas investment destination for Chinese companies.

Washington needs to develop a strategic blueprint to avoid a rupture in ties and guide Chinese [investment] toward acceptable sectors.

It can come as no surprise, then, that at the recent US-China Security and Economic Dialogue—the highest-level bilateral forum to discuss Sino-American relations—the value of the renminbi was overshadowed by an issue higher on the Chinese agenda: a push for more US market access, particularly in the high tech sector. As China's Vice Finance Minister Zhu Guangyao put it: 'We hope that the US will provide a healthy legal and institutional setting for investment by Chinese companies. In particular, we hope that the US will not discriminate against state-owned companies.'

US Concerns About Chinese Investments

Easier said than done. The United States, citing national security concerns, has shown a queasiness toward Chinese investment that has doomed past corporate acquisitions. Oil company CNOOC's [China National Offshore Oil Corporation] efforts to buy Unocal, and telecoms giant Huawei's attempt to own $_3$Com and $_3$Leaf, collapsed in the face of vociferous US opposition to placing valuable resources and technologies in Chinese hands. This led to more verbal grenades: The US Congress raised red flags about other, similar investment deals, and Beijing criticized discriminatory and opaque investment policies.

These disputes will only heat up as the US financial sector recovers and expands its credit base, and more Chinese cash from more technologically adept Chinese companies floods into the United States in search of higher corporate profits and access to technology. US natural resources, human resources, and sales will become the targets of increasing competition from Beijing. The US business community may well demand action from Washington to protect its interests. At the same time, local US authorities, who until now have welcomed investment in a desperate struggle for new sources of capital and jobs, may increasingly confront federal objections to the Chinese moves. All this would put real pressure on bilateral relations.

Washington needs to develop a strategic blueprint to avoid a rupture in ties and guide Chinese FDI toward acceptable sectors. Such a policy would clarify any differences between investment from state-owned enterprises with direct government links and that from private companies. It would balance local government needs for investment with federal government regulation and strategic considerations. It would identify opportunities and industries for joint technological development. And it would provide incentives to attract Chinese investment to those sectors in which it is wanted.

The right policy would further integrate China into the global economy and provide US jobs without threatening national security—a win-win situation that would also boost Sino-American collaboration.

The 2011 US-China Summit Made Progress

John Pomfret

John Pomfret is an Asia correspondent for The Washington Post.

Chinese President Hu Jintao's just-concluded [January 21, 2011] summit with President [Barack] Obama was a win both for the Communist Party and for Hu himself, demonstrating once again the Chinese government's reliance on ceremony to bolster its standing among its people. China's state-run newspapers ran enormous photographs of Hu with Obama, a not-so-subtle message that China is now the United States' equal on the world stage.

For the Obama administration, the meeting went smoothly and yielded some progress on difficult issues—but it also served as a reminder that the U.S.-China relationship will continue to be among Washington's most nettlesome.

Some Successes

"The most important thing they did was, for the time being, put a floor under the relationship after a very bad year," said Michael Green, a former National Security Council senior official. "No one expected a transformational summit, but if you graded it pass-fail, I say they passed."

The Chinese side, as it often does during summits, brought its checkbook, inking deals for aircraft and other heavy machinery, agricultural products and software that could be worth $45 billion for U.S. firms.

China also indicated that it would give U.S. companies better treatment and do more to protect their intellectual property. And on the hot-button issues of human rights and North Korea, the Chinese side showed a small amount of flexibility, which U.S. officials interpreted as a good sign.

There was little progress on the Obama administration's goal of pushing China to allow the value of its currency to rise—which would potentially make U.S. exports more attractive.

In addition, the Obama administration succeeded in righting what many in the administration saw to be an error during the last U.S.-China summit, in Beijing in November 2009—the United States' acknowledgment of China's "core interests" in Tibet and Taiwan. That term figured prominently in a joint statement issued in 2009. It was not repeated in the communique released Wednesday.

More broadly, Obama and other members of his Cabinet seem to have succeeded in conveying a message to China that they had no intention of backing down in the face of China's aggressive foreign policy over the past 18 months. "The administration wanted to make China understand that it needed to rein in its irrational exuberance," said Daniel Kliman, a visiting fellow at the Center for a New American Security, "that it would stand firm when necessary."

More Symbolism than Substance

In the balance between symbolism and substance, symbolism prevailed.

There was little progress on the Obama administration's goal of pushing China to allow the value of its currency to rise—which would potentially make U.S. exports more attractive. Many of the economic deals and commitments will take months or years to carry through. And on the issues of uniting to stop nuclear programs in Iran and North Korea, the two sides continue to differ on tactics and, indeed, strategy, although the two Koreas agreed this week to hold high-level military talks, a step both China and the United States support.

Hu, who left Washington on Thursday and traveled to Chicago for events to highlight the study of Mandarin and China's investments in the United States, spent the summit sticking closely to his script and Chinese bromides about "partnership based on mutual respect and benefit." At a speech Thursday sponsored by the National Committee on United States-China Relations, Hu reiterated the perennial vow of Chinese leaders that "China will never seek hegemony or seek an expansionist policy."

The one moment when he seemed to veer from his talking points occurred . . . during a news conference with Obama when he acknowledged that "a lot still needs to be done in China, in terms of human rights." Those comments were excised from his remarks in reports by the Chinese state-run press. And . . . Hu seemed to water down that acknowledgment, telling the National Committee on United States-China Relations that "we still have a long way to go before we achieve all of our development goals."

A Good Visit for President Hu

Still, the Chinese pronounced themselves satisfied with the visit.

"The two presidents had extensive and friendly exchanges," Vice Foreign Minister Cui Tiankai told reporters Wednesday after the state dinner. The visit, he said, "proved to be a great success."

For Hu, the state visit, coming late in his second term as China's top Communist Party official, was critical to his legacy and whatever ambitions he might have to continue to influence the course of Chinese politics.

The last time Hu visited the White House, he was accused of torture by a follower of China's banned Falun Gong religious sect. The White House announcer then told the audience that they were about to hear the national anthem of "the Republic of China"—the name for China's nemesis, Taiwan. And President George W. Bush didn't offer him a state dinner, just a lunch. While the Chinese side insisted on calling the meeting a "state visit," the Bush administration demurred, referring to it as a less important, "official" one.

Four years later, Hu finally obtained the treatment from the United States that he and his government have been seeking—a full-fledged state visit, complete with 21-gun salute and a banquet at the White House, although Hu did not conform to Western tradition by wearing a tuxedo. And this time there were no significant gaffes.

Since 2001, Hu has served as Chinese president and chairman of the Communist Party often in the shadow of his predecessor, Jiang Zemin, who 13 years ago was the last Chinese president to wrangle a state visit out of the United States. Now as Hu looks to leave the presidency in 2012, he can return to China having matched Jiang's feat. And for China, the visit—and the praise heaped on it by Obama—was an affirmation of its arrival as a power on the world stage.

"The United States recognized that China is a great power," Kliman said. "Hu could take that home as his legacy."

Congressional Reactions

Hu's meetings on Capitol Hill . . . did not go as swimmingly as his engagement with Obama. Some lawmakers were looking for immediate results from China, while others took the long view.

Sen. John F. Kerry (D-Mass.), chairman of the Foreign Relations Committee, emphasized the positive after his Hu huddle, suggesting that a major breakthrough had occurred in

Hu's recognition that his nation had a subpar human rights record and that key progress was achieved in making China engage other nations.

Kerry singled out Hu's assurances that China wants to defuse the nuclear crisis on the Korean Peninsula, as well as other "conflict areas." This is a different posture than the traditional Chinese view that outside nations should not meddle in China's internal affairs, nor would it meddle in others'.

"I think there's a change and a shift in their recognition of the role they need to play," Kerry told reporters. "The role of major power is not something they've been accustomed to playing."

On the House side, however, Democrats and Republicans both felt that not much progress had been made, noting that Hu engaged in a Senate-style filibuster, speaking for 20 minutes in response to a question from House Speaker John A. Boehner (R-Ohio) about trade and intellectual property.

Kerry summed up the feelings of many, though, saying that despite his optimism: "Words as we all know don't define a policy. It's going to have to be translated" into action.

Would a Stronger Renminbi Narrow the US-China Trade Imbalance?

Matthew Higgins and Thomas Klitgaard

Matthew Higgins is an assistant professor of strategic manage-ment at the business school of the Georgia Institute of Technol-ogy. Thomas Klitgaard is vice president of the international re-search office of the US Federal Reserve Bank of New York.

The United States buys much more from China than it sells to China—an imbalance that accounts for almost half of our overall merchandise trade deficit. China's policy of keeping its exchange rate low is often cited as a key driver of that country's large overall trade surplus and of its bilateral surplus with the United States. The argument is that a stronger renminbi (the official currency of China) would help reduce that country's trade imbalance with the United States by lowering the prices of U.S. goods relative to those made in China. In this post, we examine the thinking behind this view. We find that a stronger renminbi would have a relatively small near-term impact on the U.S. bilateral trade deficit with China and an even more modest impact on the overall U.S. deficit.

Our discussion focuses first on how the appreciation of the renminbi would affect U.S. imports of Chinese goods and then on how it would affect U.S. exports to China. The recent behavior of U.S. imports from and exports to China is shown in the chart below [not shown]. To close the gap between

Matthew Higgins and Thomas Klitgaard, "Would a Stronger Renminbi Narrow the US-China Trade Imbalance?," Federal Reserve Bank of New York Liberty Street Economics blog, July 13, 2011. The views expressed in this article are those of the authors and do not necessarily reflect the position of the Federal Reserve Bank of New York of the Federal Reserve System. Matthew Higgins is a vice president in the Emerging Markets and International Affairs Group of the Federal Reserve Bank of New York; Thomas Klitgaard is Vice President and Function Head, International Research Function, Federal Reserve Bank of New York. Reproduced by permission.

them, a stronger renminbi would need to markedly raise U.S. exports and/or lower U.S. imports. Although we do not believe that this adjustment is likely in the near term, we close with some observations on why the bilateral balance can be expected to shrink over the long run—owing largely to forces other than the renminbi.

While a stronger renminbi is unlikely to reduce imports, it would *provide a clear boost to U.S. export revenues;—by making U.S. products cheaper in the Chinese market.*

U.S. Imports

The structure of Chinese export production limits the impact of renminbi appreciation on U.S. spending for Chinese goods. A large proportion of China's exports consist of finished goods fashioned from imported parts and components, most often sourced from elsewhere in Asia. Recent estimates place the domestic content of China's exports at only about 50 percent. For Chinese exporters, a stronger renminbi *lowers* the domestic currency cost of imported inputs, which are typically priced in dollars. As a result, the dollar price of Chinese goods can rise less than the move in the currency without reducing profit margins. For example, given a 10 percent appreciation of the renminbi against the dollar, an exporter that sources half of its inputs from outside China could maintain profit margins with only a 5 percent hike in dollar prices. (This simple example assumes that imported input prices are unchanged in dollar terms.) The increase in dollar prices from a stronger renminbi would be even smaller if Chinese exporters decided to accept lower profit margins in order to maintain market share.

Moreover, the impact of higher dollar prices for Chinese goods might well be to *raise* the U.S. import bill. In particular,

U.S. spending on Chinese goods would rise unless higher prices induced a *proportionately larger* decline in import volumes. For example, if a 10 percent rise in the price of Chinese products resulted in only a 7 percent decline in the volume purchased, spending would rise by roughly 3 percent. Significantly, empirical studies have been as likely to find that higher prices raise U.S. import spending as lower it. Regardless of the direction of the spending impact, these offsetting price and volume effects imply that the impact of a Chinese currency appreciation on U.S. import spending would be small.

Finally, the impact of a stronger renminbi on U.S. imports would be limited by the fact that most goods purchased from China come from industries in which U.S. producers no longer have a substantial presence. Indeed, out of more than 400 detailed production categories, 60 categories account for some 80 percent of U.S. purchases from China. The same 60 categories account for less than 15 percent of U.S. manufacturing shipments. With little U.S. capacity at the ready, higher Chinese import prices might be more likely to spur increased imports from Korea or Vietnam than increased U.S. production. If so, a smaller U.S. trade deficit with China would be offset by larger deficits with other countries.

U.S. Exports

While a stronger renminbi is unlikely to reduce imports, it *would* provide a clear boost to U.S. export revenues—by making U.S. products cheaper in the Chinese market. For exports, the price and volume effects would not work at cross purposes. Studies have found that U.S. exporters leave dollar prices roughly unchanged when the value of the dollar drops against other currencies. An *unchanged* dollar price translates into a reduction in the price in foreign currency terms, boosting U.S. competitiveness, sales volume, and revenues.

Even so, the impact on the trade balance with China would be limited by the small scale of U.S. exports to China relative to imports, as we see in the chart above [not shown]. In 2010, U.S. sales to China totaled roughly $90 billion, easily a new high. However, purchases from China came to roughly $360 billion, for a bilateral deficit of around $270 billion. Suppose that a 20 percent revaluation of the renminbi relative to the dollar were to give a 20 percent boost in U.S. sales to China— roughly the effect typically found in empirical studies. The result would be to increase sales to China by a little less than $20 billion, leaving the bilateral deficit at roughly $250 billion. Even an export response twice as large as that would leave the bilateral deficit at $230 billion. The impact of a stronger renminbi appears smaller still when set against last year's aggregate U.S. merchandise trade deficit of $650 billion.

Our bottom line is that a stronger Chinese currency would not make a meaningful near-term difference in the U.S. bilateral deficit with China.

The Bilateral Deficit over the Long Run

As we have seen, U.S. imports from China currently exceed U.S. sales to China by a factor of 4 to 1. The implication of this ratio is that exports to China need to grow four times faster than imports merely to prevent the bilateral trade gap from widening. Can the bilateral trade deficit ever shrink, given this daunting math?

Yes, we think that the gap will shrink—but primarily as a consequence of the high rate of economic growth in China. We have already seen U.S. exports to China grow at a 20 to 30 percent pace in recent years, driven by the rapid expansion of that country's middle class and the resulting increase in demand for higher-end goods and services. We expect a similar pace of export growth for some time. A stronger renminbi could play an important supporting role in this process, even if it would not be the main driver. At the same time, the current share of Chinese goods in overall U.S. non-oil import spending—about 25 percent—is already so high that Chinese

175

producers will find it increasingly challenging to make further gains in market share. Within a few years, growth in U.S. purchases from China is likely to settle at the much lower rate of growth seen in overall U.S. import spending.

Disclaimer The views expressed in this post are those of the author(s) and do not necessarily reflect the position of the Federal Reserve Bank of New York or the federal Reserve System. Any errors or omissions are the responsibility of the author(s).

Both China and the United States Need to Rebalance Their Economies

Joshua Meltzer

Joshua Meltzer is a fellow with the Global Economy and Development Program of the Brookings Institution, a nonprofit public policy organization based in Washington, DC.

The latest U.S. trade figures contain some good news for the U.S., in the short term at least. In 2010, the U.S. trade deficit was $497.8 billion, which is up from $374.9 billion in 2009 but still almost 30 percent below the 2008 trade deficit of $698.8 billion. The 2010 trade balance comprised a trade in goods deficit of $646.5 billion and a trade in services surplus of $148.7 billion. While exports of goods were up $222.1 billion over 2009, imports were up $352.4 billion. Exports of services were also up $40.5 billion in 2010 compared to the increase in services imports of $23.8 billion.

If we look more closely at the U.S. import figures, we see that in 2010 imports of capital goods and industrial goods (excluding oil) were up almost 25 percent from the previous year, from approximately $643 billion in 2009 to almost $800 billion. Moreover, imports of consumer goods also increased, but relatively less, from $428.4 billion in 2009 to $483.3 billion in 2010.

The Good News

Where is the good news? First, the trade deficit is evidence of growing U.S. and global demand. The composition of U.S. imports also points to growth being driven by investment,

Joshua Meltzer, "The US Trade Deficit, China and the Need to Rebalance Growth," Brookings Institution, February 14, 2011. Copyright © 2012 The Brookings Institution. Reproduced by permission.

which should flow through to output and jobs. The increase in consumption of consumer goods is also good for the U.S. economy, as it demonstrates growing consumer confidence which should in turn give businesses the confidence to invest and create new jobs.

The growth in U.S. exports is similarly good news. The 20 percent increase in exports in 2010 occurred across a range of sectors, including hi-tech goods, automotives and agriculture products. This demonstrates growing overseas demand for export-orientated industries, which should improve the growth and jobs prospects in these sectors. This is also important for [President Barack] Obama's goal of doubling U.S. exports by 2015.

A rebalancing of Chinese growth toward domestic consumption . . . could increase demand for U.S. exports and reduce the need for China to purchase U.S. debt. This would in turn reduce the U.S.-China trade deficit.

From a macroeconomic perspective, the U.S. trade deficit is a function of the gap between national savings and investment. As U.S. savings have been unable to fund investment needs, capital from overseas has been needed, causing capital account surpluses and corresponding current account deficits. While this savings-investment imbalance remains, the U.S. will continue to run current account deficits. Since 2000, the shortfall in U.S. savings has become increasingly driven by the need to finance U.S. budget deficits. The U.S. budget went from a surplus in 2000 of 2.4 percent of GDP [gross domestic product, a measure of a country's total economic output] to a deficit in 2003 of 3.3 percent, and the Congressional Budget Office has predicted that the budget deficit will reach 9.8 percent of GDP in 2011. The need to fund budget deficits from national savings has contributed to the trade deficits.

The U.S.-China Trade Relationship

These trade figures also demonstrate the significance of the U.S.-China trading relationship. In 2010, the U.S.-China trade deficit increased to over $273 billion, the highest bilateral trade deficit on record. It represents almost 55 percent of the total U.S. trade deficit. The U.S.-China trade deficit is linked to the undervaluation of the renmimbi (RMB) [China's currency] which is a result of it being pegged to the U.S. dollar. Like all cheap assets, the RMB's undervaluation has led to excess demand for Chinese goods (in the form of imports), and for the RMB to pay for these goods. To meet this demand for the RMB and to maintain the peg, the Chinese government has had to supply more of its currency by purchasing low yielding U.S. Treasury bonds. China currently holds almost $900 billion in US Treasury securities.

The peg has had a range of consequences for the Chinese economy. One of these has been an over allocation of resources to China's export industry and a corresponding lack of investment and development of its non-tradable sectors, in particular its services sector. It has also reduced the Chinese government's control over its monetary policy because increases in its interest rates would only increase demand for the RMB, forcing China to supply even more RMB to maintain the peg with the dollar. The need to supply RMB to maintain the peg has also contributed to inflationary pressures in China, which is pushing 5 percent.

At the G-20 [referring to a group of the world industrialized nations] Summit in Seoul in November [2010], members pledged to "undertake policies to support private savings and where appropriate, undertake fiscal consolidation while maintaining open markets and strengthening export sectors. Members with sustained, significant external surpluses pledge[d] to strengthen domestic sources of growth". Consistent with this agreement, a rebalancing of Chinese growth toward domestic consumption, combined with movement toward a freely floating RMB and liberalization of its capital account, should lead to a rebalancing of the Chinese economy that could increase demand for U.S. exports and reduce the need for the China to purchase U.S. debt. This would in turn reduce the U.S.-China trade deficit.

A rebalancing only of the Chinese economy, however, will not be enough to address the U.S. trade deficit. Without a corresponding rebalancing over time of the U.S. economy toward less consumption and more savings, we can expect to see continuing U.S. trade deficits.

Organizations to Contact

The editors have compiled the following list of organizations concerned with the issues debated in this book. The descriptions are derived from materials provided by the organizations. All have publications or information available for interested readers. The list was compiled on the date of publication of the present volume; the information provided here may change. Be aware that many organizations take several weeks or longer to respond to inquiries, so allow as much time as possible.

China Daily
6/F, B3 Tower, Ziguang Building, No. 11 Huixin Dongjie
Chaoyang District   100029, PRC
   Beijing
+86 (10) 84883300
website: www.chinadaily.com.cn

China Daily is an English-language newspaper published in China. The newspaper is controlled by the Chinese government and reflects official policy. *China Daily* was one of the first Chinese newspapers to have an online presence. Its website provides up-to-the-minute, in-depth news and information about Chinese politics, economy, culture, entertainment, and lifestyle. It also covers international news and provides in-depth analysis through columnists, opinions, and editorials. Searches of the website lead the reader to a wealth of articles and news reports about US-China trade.

Food & Water Watch
1616 P Street NW, Suite 300, Washington, DC   20036
(202) 683-2500 • fax: (202) 683-2501
website: www.foodandwaterwatch.org

Food & Water Watch is a watchdog group that monitors government standards and oversight of the safety of food and water, challenges the corporate control and abuse of food and water resources, and provides information to the public about these important issues. A search of its website produces press releases, articles, and alerts concerning the safety of Chinese food imports. Two recent examples are: *Chinese Consumers Send a Warning* and a fact sheet, *Chinese Imports.*

International Trade Administration (ITA)

US Department of Commerce, 1401 Constitution Ave. NW
Washington, DC   20230
(800) 872-8723
website: http://trade.gov

Part of the US Department of Commerce, ITA's mission is to create prosperity by strengthening the competitiveness of US industry, promoting trade and investment, and ensuring fair trade and compliance with trade laws and agreements. The agency's website provides information about US international trade policy, including trade statistics, press releases, speeches, and an online bookstore that provides access to various agency reports and studies. A search of the website produces numerous government publications on trading with China.

John L. Thornton China Center

Brookings Institution, 1775 Massachusetts Ave. NW
Washington, DC   20036
(202) 797-6000
website: www.brookings.edu/china.aspx

The John L. Thornton China Center is a project of the Brookings Institution, a think tank that conducts research and education in the areas of foreign policy, economics, government, and the social sciences. The Center provides research, analysis, and dialogue focusing on China's emergence and the implications of this for the United States, China's neighbors, and the rest of the world. Its website features numerous publications on China, including *Managing the China Challenge: How to Achieve Corporate Success in the People's Republic* and *The Renminbi: The Political Economy of a Currency.*

United Nations Conference on Trade
and Development (UNCTAD)
Palais des Nations, 8-14, Av. de la Paix, Geneva 10   1211
   Switzerland
+41 22 917 1234 • fax: +41 22 917 0057
e-mail: info@unctad.org
website: www.unctad.org

The United Nations Conference on Trade and Development
(UNCTAD) was established by the United Nations (UN) to
help integrate developing countries into the world economy.
UNCTAD has addressed China's growing importance in the
world economy in a number of informative analyses and publications, including *Key Issues in China's Economic Transformation, Trade and Development Report 2005*, which examines the
underlying forces of China as a key player in the world
economy, and *Trade and Development Report 2006*, which dis-
cusses the implications of different ways of correcting the existing global imbalances.

US Census Bureau Foreign Trade
US Census Bureau, 4600 Silver Hill Rd.
Washington, DC   20233
(301) 763-4636
e-mail: pio@census.gov
website: www.census.gov/foreign-trade

Part of the US Census Bureau, the Foreign Trade division is a
government agency that compiles and disseminates statistical
information about US trade. Among other publications, the
division produces the *Guide to Foreign Trade Statistics*, which
offers statistics on imports and exports on a country-by-
country basis.

The US-China Business Council (USCBC)
1818 N St. NW, Suite 200, Washington, DC   20036
(202) 429-0340 • fax: (202) 775-2476
e-mail: info@uschina.org
website: www.uschina.org

The US-China Business Council (USCBC) is a private, non-profit organization of more than two hundred and fifty American corporations that do business with China. Its mission is to expand the United States's commercial relationship with China to the benefit of the US economy. USCBC advocates a balanced approach to trade with China—one that expands opportunities while identifying and removing trade barriers. This website features a wide variety of statistical and policy reports, analyses, and other publications relevant to US-China trade relations.

**US-China Economic and Security
Review Commission (USCC)**
444 North Capitol St. NW, Suite 602, Washington, DC   20001
(202) 624-1407
e-mail: contact@uscc.gov
website: www.uscc.gov

The US-China Economic and Security Review Commission was created in 2000 to monitor, investigate, and submit to Congress an annual report on the national security implications of the bilateral trade and economic relationship between the United States and the People's Republic of China, and to provide recommendations, where appropriate, to Congress for legislative and administrative action. The Commission's website offers a great deal of substantive information concerning the bilateral trade and economic relationship between the United States and China and outlines legislative and administrative action taken by Congress. Publications include annual reports to Congress, transcripts of Congressional hearings and testimony, research papers, and press releases. Recent research, for example, includes Backgrounder: China's 12th Five-Year Plan and Potential Health & Safety Impacts from Pharmaceuticals and Supplements Containing Chinese-Sourced Raw Ingredient.

US-China Policy Foundation
316 Pennsylvania Ave. SE, Suites 201-202
Washington, DC   20003

(202) 547-8615 • fax: (202) 547-8853
e-mail: uscpf@uscpf.org
website: www.uscpf.org

The US-China Policy Foundation is a nonpartisan, nonprofit, nonadvocacy educational organization devoted to broadening awareness of China and US-China relations in the US policy community. The group publishes a biannual report called the *Washington Journal of Modern China* and a newsletter entitled *US-China Policy Review*, which are available at its website. It also produces *China Forum*, an educational television program devoted exclusively to China.

US Consumer Product Safety Commission (CPSC)
4330 East West Highway, Bethesda, MD   20814
(301) 504-7923
website: www.cpsc.gov

The US Consumer Product Safety Commission is charged with protecting the public from unreasonable risks of serious injury or death from more than 15,000 types of consumer products under the agency's jurisdiction. A search of the Commission's website reveals numerous publications relating to Chinese imports, China's efforts to improve the quality and safety of its products, and various recalls by the Commission of goods manufactured in China.

US Food and Drug Administration (FDA)
10903 New Hampshire Ave., Silver Spring, MD   20993
(888) 463-6332
website: www.fda.gov

The FDA is responsible for protecting the public health by assuring the safety, efficacy, and security of human and veterinary drugs, biological products, medical devices, our nation's food supply, cosmetics, and products that emit radiation. A search of the FDA website produces a wealth of information—testimony, news articles, transcripts of press conferences, reports, and other publications—relevant to the issue of Chinese food and drug imports, China's trade policies, and actions being taken by the US government to ensure safe imports.

World Bank
1818 H St. NW, Washington, DC 20433
(202) 473-1000 • fax: (202) 477-6391
website: www.worldbank.org

The World Bank seeks to reduce poverty and improve the standards of living of poor people around the world. It promotes sustainable growth and investments in developing countries through loans, technical assistance, and policy guidance. The World Bank website contains a section on China that offers a variety of resources on the country and its economic rise to power. These include a country overview, a country brief (which summarizes recent developments, future challenges, and bank assistance to China), and numerous free publications. One of the available publications is *China Quarterly Update*, which reports on the country's economic status.

World Trade Organization (WTO)
Centre William Rappard, Rue de Lausanne 154
Geneva 21   CH-1211
   Switzerland
+41 (0)22 739 51 11 • fax: +41 (0)22 731 42 06
e-mail: enquiries@wto.org
website: www.wto.org

The World Trade Organization (WTO) is a global international organization whose purpose is to facilitate free trade among nations. The WTO publishes trade statistics, research and analysis, studies, reports, and the journal *World Trade Review*. Recent publications are available on the WTO website. The WTO website also includes a section providing information on China's participation in the WTO, including a comprehensive news archive, official documents, trade statistics, various resources and publications, explanations of numerous trade topics and terminology, as well as trade dispute cases involving China.

Bibliography

Books

Philip Andrews-Speed and Roland Dannreuther — *China, Oil and Global Politics.* New York: Routledge, 2011.

Jan Willem Blankert — *China Rising: Will the West Be Able to Cope? The Real Long-term Challenge to the Rise of China.* Hackensack, NJ: World Scientific Publishing Company, 2009.

Craig Calhoun and Georgi Derluguian — *Aftermath: A New Global Economic Order?* New York: NYU Press, 2011.

Cary Coglianese, Adam M. Finkel, and David Zaring, eds. — *Import Safety: Regulatory Governance in the Global Economy.* Philadelphia: University of Pennsylvania Press, 2009.

Ian Fletcher and Edward Luttwak — *Free Trade Doesn't Work: What Should Replace It and Why.* Washington, DC: US Business & Industry Council, 2010.

Yuning Gao — *China as the Workshop of the World: An Analysis at the National and Industrial Level of China in the International Division of Labor.* New York: Routledge, 2011.

Morris Goldstein and Nicholas R. Lardy — *Debating China's Exchange Rate Policy.* Washington, DC: Peterson Institute, 2008.

Ian Jeffries | *Economic Developments in Contemporary China: A Guide.* New York: Routledge, 2010.

Paul Midler | *Poorly Made in China: An Insider's Account of the Tactics Behind China's Production Game.* Hoboken, NJ: Wiley, 2009.

Wayne M. Morrison | *China–US Trade Issues.* Washington, DC: Congressional Research Service, 2011.

Peter W. Navarro and Greg Autry | *Death by China: Confronting the Dragon—A Global Call to Action.* Upper Saddle River, NJ: Pearson Prentice Hall, 2011.

Benjamin I. Page and Tao Xie | *Living with the Dragon: How the American Public Views the Rise of China.* New York: Columbia University Press, 2010.

Gary Schmitt | *The Rise of China: Essays on the Future Competition.* Jackson, TN: Encounter Books, 2009.

Susan L. Shirk | *China, Fragile Superpower: How China's Internal Politics Could Derail Its Peaceful Rise.* New York: Oxford University Press, 2008.

Arvind Subramanian | *Eclipse: Living in the Shadow of China's Economic Dominance.* Washington, DC: Institute of International Economics, 2011.

Christopher Torrens	*Doing Business in China: A Guide to the Risks and the Rewards.* Hoboken, NJ: Wiley, 2010.
Linda Yueh	*The Future of Asian Trade and Growth: Economic Development with the Emergence of China.* New York: Routledge, 2010.

Periodicals & Internet Sources

Mary Amiti and Caroline Freund	"China's Export Boom," *Finance and Development*, Vol. 44, No. 3, September 2007.
The Associated Press	"China to Enact New Product Safety Rules in Bid to Restore Its Reputation," *International Herald-Tribune*, March 5, 2008.
The Associated Press	"China Urges US to Balance Trade by Allowing More High Tech Exports," *The Huffington Post*, May 10, 2011. www.huffingtonpost.com.
Michael Babad	"A Trade War Remains a 'Significant Threat,'" *The Globe and Mail*, February 7, 2011.
David Barboza	"Inflation in China Poses Big Threat to Global Trade," *The New York Times*, April 17, 2011.
Heda Bayron	"US–China Economic Relations: Win-Lose or Win-Win?," *Voice of America*, January 11, 2011.

Ben Blanchard | "China Says Product Safety Push a Complete Success," Reuters.com, January 14, 2008. www.reuters.com.

Massimo Calabresi | "Hu's Visit: Can Timothy Geithner Prevent a US–China Trade War?," *Time*, January 20, 2011.

Molly Castelazo | "China Owns a Lot of Debt. Why?," FutureofUSChinaTrade.com, July 24, 2011. www.futureofuschinatrade.com.

Patrick Corcoran | "US Product Safety Agency Targets Chinese Goods with New Office in Beijing," *FairWarning*, January 10, 2011. www.fairwarning.org.

Jacob Goldstein | "The US Owes China $1.2 Trillion," *Planet Money*, March 1, 2011. www.npr.org/blogs/money.

Alexandra Harney | "The Last Days of Cheap Chinese," *Slate*, April 8, 2008. www.slate.com.

Joseph Lazzaro | "The Untold Story of the US Trade Deficit: Rising Exports," *Daily Finance*, February 16, 2011.

John Lee | "Paper Tiger: China's No Threat to the US," *Business Week*, February 26, 2010.

Mitch Lipka | "China Imports in the Grocery Store: A Cause for Concern," Reuters.com, May 11, 2011. http://blogs.reuters.com.

Walter Lohman — "More Charm than Harm: Lessons from China's Economic Offensive in Southeast Asia," The Heritage Foundation, February 24, 2010. www.heritage.org.

Pew Research Center for the People & the Press — "Strengthen Ties with China, but Get Tough on Trade," January 12, 2011. http://pewresearch.org.

Bob Pisani — "China Imports Costing More: Days of 'Cheap Items' Over?," *CNBC*, February 15, 2008. www.cnbc.com.

Catherine Rampell — "'Made in China,' but Still Profiting Americans," *The New York Times*, August 15, 2011.

Henry Rosemont, Jr. — "Is China a Threat?," *Foreign Policy in Focus*, February 6, 2008.

Mark Trumbull — "How Much Does US–China Trade Hurt American Workers? Slowly, a Clearer Picture," *Christian Science Monitor*, May 10, 2011.

Todd Wallack — "Drug Makers Stick by China," *The Boston Globe*, March 14, 2008.

Mark Weisbrot — "2016: When China Overtakes the US," *The Guardian*, April 27, 2011.

Elizabeth Weise and Julie Schmit — "FDA Limits Chinese Food Additive Imports," *USA Today*, April 30, 2007.

Mathew Yglesias   "'Made In China' Accounts for Less than 3 Percent of American Personal Consumption Expenditures," ThinkProgress.org, August 9, 2011. http://thinkprogress.org.

Index

Trade
    balanced trade, 44–46, 103–104
    Chinese policies of, 18, 54–56
    of computers/electronic equipment, 38, 40–41, 44
    foreign, 118–119
    globalization and, 56, 117
    US policy for, 133–134
    See also Free-trade; United States (US)-China trade; United States (US)-China trade deficit; World Trade Organization (WTO)
Trumbull, Mark, 118–122

U

United States (US)
    balanced economy in, 177–180
    Chinese investments in, 151–152, 163–166
    Chinese State Owned Enterprises, subsidies, 152, 153–162
    economic policy/strategy of, 102, 120–122
    as economic superpower, 118–122
    foreign-owned companies in, 106–107
    free-trade policy, 105, 107, 121, 133–134
    laissez faire policies of, 99, 100, 103
    multipolar global economy and, 120
    oil dependence by, 121
    overview, 118
    tariff usage by, 103, 109–110, 114
    tax losses by, 107–108
United States (US), exports
    to China, 54, 111, 136
    Chinese inflation impact on, 41, 172–174
    cost of, 145
    jobs from, 43–45
    loss of, 38, 48
    made in USA goods, 144
    overview, 174–175
    strength of, 36, 46–47, 110
    value of, 23, 90–91, 113, 168, 177–178
United States (US), imports
    benefits of, 28–33, 113–114
    Chinese yuan impact on, 172–174
    consumer driven, 28–33, 112–113
    gross domestic product (GDP) and, 29, 32, 90, 101, 151, 178
    growth of, 20–21
    non-oil imports, 39
    overview, 19–20, 173–174
    See also Chinese imports to US
United States (US)-China trade
    agricultural concerns over, 139, 167, 178
    benefits of, 139–140
    bilateral investment treaty, 132, 136
    China, benefit from, 35–36
    China, unfair practices over, 91–92
    China's currency manipulation in, 146–147
    competition with, 142–145